The American House

The American House is an illustrated survey of 100 iconic houses in the United States, from the thirteenth century to the present day. The selection ranges from the dwellings of the indigenous population, through the diverse houses of America's pan-European settlers and Modernist masterpieces of the twentieth century, to today's contemporary creations. This exciting collection covers all key movements, styles and regions, including the mud houses of the Tiwa Indians, the pioneering homes of the Chicago School, the minimalism of the International Style and eco designs by today's architects. America's best-known architects are featured through their landmark houses, such as Thomas Jefferson's Monticello, Frank Lloyd Wright's Fallingwater, Pierre Koenig's Stahl House and Rick Joy's Tubac House, alongside groundbreaking designs by lesser-known architects. Organized chronologically, each house is represented by a full-page image and explanatory text. ***The American House*** is an essential guide to the pioneering history of American domestic architecture.

Cliff Palace Pueblo Indians

Cliff Palace, the spectacular, prehistoric 200-room village carved into steep stone cliffs in Colorado, has long been a source of wonder. The Pueblo Indians are thought to have occupied the canyon country we now call Mesa Verde since AD 300; however, the magnificent and mysterious carved cliff dwellings are estimated to date from around AD 1200. They were occupied only for a mere one hundred years and were abandoned for centuries. The remarkable Cliff Palace and other cliff dwellings were made by excavating around caves and other openings and adding rooms — typically 2 m x 3 m (6 ft x 9 ft) — of sandstone block with mortar made of mud and water. These monumental structures remained undiscovered by the western world until W H Jackson, a famous pioneer photographer, came upon them in 1874. Thanks to the USA National Park system, Mesa Verde and its cliff dwellings have been preserved as a national park since 1906.

Cliff Palace, Mesa Verde National Park, Canyon de Chelly, CO, circa AD 1100–1300. **Pueblo Indians**. Active USA, circa AD 300–1300.

Taos Pueblo Tiwa Indians

When the Spanish conquistadors occupied these Native American settlements in the mid-sixteenth century, they described them as *pueblos* (villages). Today, thirty *pueblos* survive in Arizona and New Mexico, some as much as a thousand years old. The main part of these buildings were most likely constructed between AD 1000 and 1450. Taos,

below the Sangre de Cristo Mountains, is the largest of these, comprising two clusters of dwellings. Up to five storeys high, the stepped blocks house some 1,500 Tiwa-speaking people. Entry to the dwellings was formerly through openings in the roofs, the ladders being drawn up afterwards. Today they have doors and windows in the

mud-plastered adobe walls, with *vigas* (roof-poles) extending from them. Un-named and multi-functional, the rooms are used differently according to the season. Outside there are domed ovens for baking and, hidden from view, the *kivas* or underground ceremonial chambers essential to the annual cycle of fertility dances and rituals.

Taos Pueblo, Taos, NM, AD 1000 – 1450, still occupied today. **Tiwa Indians**. Active USA, thirteenth century to present day.

Earth Lodge Mandan Indians

A large, round, Mandan earth lodge, built on a framework of four sturdy posts and willow branches and covered with thick grass mats and earth, might measure up to 15 m (50 ft) in diameter and house twenty to thirty people. Mandan women gathered the building materials from their native Missouri River Valley (an area now part of North Dakota) and built the lodges. The women also owned, maintained and inherited the dwellings, along with any family land. A typical Mandan village consisted of more than one hundred lodges built in a circle around a sacred cedar tree or cedar post. The dwellings disappeared after the Mandan Indians were almost eradicated by smallpox in the 1830s, although reconstructions were made based on first-hand accounts and sketches from surviving Mandan and on the detailed paintings of American artist-adventurers, such as George Catlin.

Earth Lodge, Missouri River Valley, ND, as built c1500–1838. **Mandan Indians of North America**. Active USA, c8000 BC to present day.

6

Allen House Thomas Bardwell

With its symmetrical front facade and asymmetrical roof sloping to the rear, the Allen House is typical of its time (colonial America) and place (New England). Historians believe this house to have been built by Thomas Bardwell in 1722, later passing on to a succession of his family members. The Saltbox has long been considered a purely American house form, but it was actually an evolution of the English Tudor cottage with an added lean-to. Rectangular in plan with two floors and an attic, the roof would be steeply pitched to the rear, sloping down almost to the ground floor. The central doorway, generally on the south-facing side, was usually flanked by two double-hung windows with a row of five windows on the first floor above. Inside, there were typically just four rooms, two per floor, each with its own hearth. Subtle regional differences exist in these generally wood-frame and clapboard houses, and in the southern states the same form was termed a Catslide house.

Allen House (originally Bardwell House), Deerfield, MA, 1722. **Thomas Bardwell**. b USA, 1691. d USA, 1781.

Mount Vernon George Washington

From this view, the field-side facade of America's most famous house, it is clear to see where George Washington lost his way when expanding the family estate into a formal seat for a country gentleman. The symmetry is askew, the oversized entry fails to line up with the cupola and the windows are disordered. Although Mount Vernon appears to be built of stone, it is in fact constructed of cut blocks of wood disguised under paint mixed with sand to create a gritty surface. However, Washington, the father of his country and the very first to assume the US presidency, made up for these shortcomings when he planned the Potomac River facade in 1787. He added a piazza and the two-storey, square-columned porch, so widely reproduced in American buildings that it is both icon and cliché. Yet, despite an overload of imitations, Mount Vernon stands as a potent symbol of national idealism: the dream house, the emblem of patriotism.

Mount Vernon, Fairfax County, VA, 1757–87. **George Washington**. b Westmoreland County, VA, 1732. d Mount Vernon, VA, 1799.

The White House James Hoban

The White House has been home and workplace to every US president, with the exception of George Washington, who commissioned the open competition for the presidential seat in 1792. James Hoban's winning Neo-Classical Georgian design, of which the central portion largely remains intact today, was based on Leinster Hall in Dublin and Plate 41 of James Gibb's *A Book of Architecture* (1728). Gutted by British soldiers during the war of 1812, the building was saved from utter destruction by a providential downpour. The familiar colonnaded north entrance and south portico, designed by Benjamin Latrobe, were faithfully reconstructed, while large-scale modernization in 1902 added wings containing offices. The white stucco facade of this surprisingly compact house masks an interior containing four staterooms and later presidential additions, such as Roosevelt's Oval Office and Clinton's jogging track.

The White House, Washington, DC, 1792–1800, rebuilt 1814–29. **James Hoban**. b Callan, Ireland, 1763. d Washington, DC, 1831.

Boscobel States Morris Dyckman

Long considered an important Federal period work of Palladian influence, Boscobel is a study in proportion and refinement. It is elegant in both its simplicity of design and its adornment, most particularly the carved wooden swags along the portico and the graceful balustrades. A descendant of the early Dutch settlers and a staunch British Loyalist, Dyckman dreamed of building an English manor house in the Hudson River Valley. Little did he know that the house would, in fact, become an outstanding example of American architecture of the period. While in London in 1800, he bought all that he would need to furnish such a house — china, crystal and silver — before the first foundation stone was even laid. But, sadly, he died quite suddenly soon after the building work started, and was never to see his dream realized. It was left to his widow, Elizabeth, to complete Boscobel, with the help of Vermilyea, a master builder and a relative.

Harrison Gray Otis House Charles Bulfinch

This was the third townhouse that Charles Bulfinch designed for his patron within the space of thirteen years. Otis was of the new, post-Revolutionary American aristocracy, a natural client for America's first native-born professional architect. Working from English models, and a nudge from Thomas Jefferson, Bulfinch set the pattern for both public and private Federal architecture, developing a national brand of Neo-Classicism that was modest yet elegant. Loftier than the earlier houses, here Bulfinch clearly separates the public area from the domestic by emphasizing the principal floor with triple-hung windows; the first to be seen in America. Bulfinch introduced architectural concepts in Boston that eventually travelled south and then west with the new nation. Most significantly, he broke the box mould of the colonial house, creating oval rooms, spiralling staircases and varying room heights, bestowing a style that came to be called 'Bulfinchian'.

Harrison Gray Otis House, Boston, MA, 1805–8. **Charles Bulfinch**. b Boston, MA, 1763. d Boston, MA, 1844.

Monticello Thomas Jefferson

Monticello is Thomas Jefferson's ode to the architecture he loved; that of Greece, Rome and Palladio's Italy. The third president of the USA, Jefferson was considered to be the country's first architect, and called Monticello his 'essay in architecture'. In the course of the forty years of its construction, he transformed the house from a one-room dwelling to a three-storey, thirty-three-room mansion. Following the death of his wife in 1784 and a trip to France, he rebuilt the house on a grander scale, influenced by European architecture, with far more elegant rooms and adding the famous entrance portico. Inside, the house is filled with his labour-saving innovations, including automatic doors and a dumb waiter. Jefferson was the first major exponent of Palladian-influenced architecture in the New World and his passion for Classicism has influenced American architecture through the centuries and still does even today.

Monticello, nr Charlottesville, VA, 1769–1809. **Thomas Jefferson**. b Shadwell, VA, 1743. d Monticello, VA, 1826.

Pioneer Farmstead John Davis

Set amid the dense woodland of this North Carolina forest, John Davis's early American log and fieldstone farmstead draws on Swedish vernacular log-building traditions. Log cabin house design originated in the northern countries of Europe and was first constructed in America by Swedish settlers in Delaware in the late 1630s; later pioneers were to build log cabins further and further west. Many Americans still lived in these primitive-type dwellings as late as 1800. Early log cabins were built as temporary dwellings, to be replaced once the pioneer community was established and permanent building materials, such as stone, were procured. Here, like other farmsteaders, Davis utilizes easily obtainable local woodland materials, aiming for minimal building costs. This pioneer-style house is sustainable organic architecture in the purest sense, reflecting economic and ecological common sense and cultural relativism.

Pioneer Farmstead, Great Smokey Mountains, NC, c1830s. **John Davis**. Active USA, nineteenth century.

Centre Family Dwelling House Micajah Burnett

The US Federal style, with its subdued ornamentation and symmetrical facade, was adopted by the religious Shaker sect which sought an architecture based on harmony and essential practicality. Shaker dwelling houses were built to accommodate hundreds of adherents, known as families, organized along spiritual rather than blood lines. While men and women lived under one roof with a communal dining room, there were separate dormitories, entrances and staircases in this environment designed to instil the tenets of their religion. Micajah Burnett, a skilful builder, applied raised mortar to the brick coursing, which added depth to the facade, while improving its impermeability. Perfection was paramount: the effulgence of light and air, the permanence of limestone and the simplicity of carved wood reflect the Shakers' asceticism, anticipating the Modernist aesthetic in design, as evidenced by the continued popularity of the style.

Centre Family Dwelling House, Pleasant Hill, KY, 1824–34. **Micajah Burnett**. b Pleasant Hill, KY, 1791. d USA, 1879.

William Roper House Robert William Roper

Built in the American Greek Revival style, William Roper House is a graceful yet imposing sight along East Battery Street in downtown Charleston. Bold, classically simple elements are found throughout the house, such as the five-column Ionic portico, interior and exterior mouldings and friezes, pediment gables, a full entablature and heavy cornices. They were often painted white to replicate the white marble Greek ruins, although these had, in fact, originally been brightly coloured. The Greek Revival style flourished in the United States — as nowhere else — during the 1830s and 40s, and expressed America's aspiration to represent the new Republic and the nation's foundation in Ancient Greek democratic ideals. Alexander Jackson Davis complained that Greek temple-front buildings were so prevalent in American towns that it was difficult for visitors to distinguish between a church, a bank or a courthouse.

William Roper House, Charleston, SC, 1838. Robert William Roper. Active USA, early to mid-nineteenth century. 15

Henry Delamater House Alexander Jackson Davis

One of more than a hundred picturesque villas designed and popularized by Alexander Jackson Davis, this eager little country house exhibits the gingerbread brackets, board-and-batten siding and bulging bays that are the signature of his Americanized reading of the 'English cottage style'. Fully realized by the mid-nineteenth century, the fashion for ornamental, romantic summer homes and village dwellings had spread across the land, their form and decoration largely influenced by, if not directly copied from, the architect's exacting drawings reproduced in contemporary pattern books and magazines. Philosophically grounded in the revolt against Classicist domestic architecture, Davis pioneered charm in its stead, creating family houses as welcoming as their verandas were elaborate. The Henry Delamater House, its overly pronounced gable at an equal height to neighbouring treetops, is tailored to its immediate landscape and orientated towards nature.

Henry Delamater House, Rhinebeck, NY, 1844. **Alexander Jackson Davis**. b New York, NY, 1803. d West Orange, NJ, 1892.

Brevard-Mmahat House James Calrow

The Brevard-Mmahat House is a tall, narrow building with a double-storey front portico supported by Corinthian columns. A cast-iron gallery, one of the first built in the area, runs along the side garden. Although officially an antebellum house, built before the outbreak of the American Civil War, a library wing was added after the war in 1869. The New Orleans Garden District was created in 1825 when a plantation was subdivided to form the town of Lafayette, later annexed by New Orleans in 1852. The houses of this now gracious neighbourhood are typified, as is seen in Brevard-Mmahat House, by galleries, broad porches and outdoor garden 'rooms'. They are, unusually, open houses with only louvred shutters protecting them. The Brevard-Mmahat House holds an additional literary distinction in that it appears as Mayfair House in several of bestselling author, Anne Rice's books, including Witching Hour.

Longwood Samuel Sloan

With a finial rising from its ornate Byzantine cupola, Longwood is the folly to end all follies. An octagonal residence of elaborate proportion, dimension and detailing, the house's eclectic mix of Corinthian fluted columns and Victorian 'Carpenter Gothic' capitals are worthy of particular note. (Carpenter Gothic is a style featuring exterior woodwork with Gothic motifs.) It was begun in 1859 with a design by the Philadelphia society architect, Samuel Sloan, and built in 1860–1 for Haller Nutt, a physician, and his wife Julia. The dates themselves are significant in that the American Civil War was by then under way, and the South was increasingly becoming a battleground. Indeed, Dr Nutt dismissed the carpenters so they could return to Pennsylvania to fight for the North, and the house was never completed. Only nine of the planned thirty-two rooms were finished, although those are still intact today, along with their original furniture.

Longwood, Natchez, MS, 1860–1. **Samuel Sloan**. b Beaver Dam, nr Honeybrook, PA, 1815. d Raleigh, NC, 1884.

18

Mark Twain House Edward Potter

The author Samuel Clemens, better known as Mark Twain, purchased two parcels of land in Hartford, an area known for its community of writers, artists and musicians. He then commissioned the popular architect Edward T Potter to design this house, which is arguably the most spectacular example of the Stick Style, so popular in America between 1860 and 1880. Loosely based on medieval architecture, the style, like Clemens himself, was unusually flamboyant, and has been described as 'the avoidance of plain walls at all costs'. It is most evident in the curving porch-support braces, the steeply-pitched gabled roof with overhanging eaves and the horizontal wall-banding raised from the surface for emphasis. As soon as funds permitted, Clemens employed the brilliant designer, Louis Comfort Tiffany (1848–1933), to decorate the interior. The result is one of the best surviving examples of Aesthetic design, a reactionary response to overblown Victorian design.

Mark Twain House, Hartford, CT, 1874. **Edward Tuckerman Potter**. b Schenectady, NY, 1831. d New York, NY, 1904.

Watts Sherman House Henry Hobson Richardson

With its extraordinary texture and balance, the Watts Sherman House alludes to America's nineteenth-century tendency to imitate historic house styles, as well as anticipating the influence of the Arts and Crafts style to come. It is arguably the first Shingle Style house, and although designed by Henry Hobson Richardson, it was at a time when Stanford White (largely considered to be the premier Shingle Style architect) was employed by the Richardson office. Indeed, Richardson recommended that White finish the interiors, and the client, Sherman, subsequently commissioned White to design the 1881 addition to the house. The building materials included stone, wood, brick and stucco, as well as the identifying shingles. The house makes strong references to early English architecture, with its large chimneys and half-timbering, and scholars believe that it was Richardson's tribute to the Revivalist English architect, Norman Shaw.

Watts Sherman House, Newport, RI, 1874–5. **Henry Hobson Richardson**. **b** Priestley Plantation, LA, 1838. **d** Brooklyn, NY, 1886.

William H Rhawn House Frank Furness

Original, bizarre (and celebrated for being both), Frank Furness was Philadelphia's architect of choice during the business and building boom following the American Civil War. He could impose his arsenal of mannerist eccentricities on the design of a suburban home as deftly as he could wield them on a downtown bank. The Rhawn House is evidence of his individualism at work: a unique, daring and personal composition of conventional architectural elements (columns, brackets, gables, arches) and ordinary materials (stone, brick, shingle, wood); his genius was in the mix. The great U-shaped porch supports and balances a pyramid of a roof that peaks in stages to a towering height. This house is different enough from the formalist nature of most contemporary houses to suggest that his innovations prefigured the later architecture of Functionalism, as in the work of Louis Sullivan, who worked as a young man in Furness's office.

William H Rhawn House, Philadelphia, PA, 1881. **Frank Furness**. **b** Philadelphia, PA, 1839. **d** Medea, PA, 1912.

William G Low House McKim Mead & White

Charles McKim designed this now-demolished house on a site overlooking Narragansett Bay for a New York lawyer living in Brooklyn. This vast, triangular house was dominated by its great gabled roof sloping close to the ground and spanning 42 m (140 ft). It was covered, top-to-bottom, in square-cut cedar shingles and had a mostly flat facade, interrupted by a series of bay windows. At one end, tucked under the gable roof, was a deep covered porch. The Beaux-Arts-trained McKim designed the interiors to be spare, with little ornamentation, but the rooms were arranged on six different levels, offering a certain amount of spatial complexity. The simplicity of the architecture gave the house a great coherence; McKim's early Shingle Style work reflected his passion for clarity and geometric order. Although it was torn down in the 1960s, scholar Richard Guy Wilson terms the Low House one of McKim Mead & White's 'most original' designs.

William G Low House, Bristol, RI, 1887 (since demolished). **Charles McKim**. b Pennsylvania, PA, 1847. d St James, NY, 1909. **William Mead**. b Brattleboro, VT, 1846. d Paris, France, 1928.
Stanford White. b New York, NY, 1853. d New York, NY, 1906.

Biltmore Richard Morris Hunt

A French Renaissance château built in the Blue Ridge Mountains of North Carolina, Biltmore holds the title as the largest private house ever constructed in the United States. Richard Morris Hunt had designed many grand mansions for some of America's richest families, but Biltmore, for George Vanderbilt (1862–1914), was by far his grandest.

The house, with a 238 m (780 ft) Indiana limestone facade, has 250 rooms, of which 34 are bedrooms, and a swimming pool, bowling alley and gym in the basement. Hunt, who was instrumental in bringing the Beaux-Arts educational system to the United States, drew on precedents from French châteaux, including Blois,

Chenonceaux and Chambord; distinct allusions to all three can be found in Biltmore's architecture, from the form of the house to the detailing of the windows. The house was fully electrified on its completion in 1895, and was among the first residences to use the new light bulbs invented by Thomas Edison.

Biltmore, Asheville, NC, 1889–95. **Richard Morris Hunt**. b Brattleboro, VT, 1827. d Newport, RI, 1895.

'Painted Ladies' Matthew Kavanaugh

Inspired by the eighteenth-century terraced row houses of London, San Francisco's townhouses were built to accommodate the thriving middle class that emerged after the California Gold Rush. Highly ornamented and brightly painted, the timber-frame structures earned the name 'Painted Ladies'. Although some were designed by well-known architects, most were prefabricated and assembled by specialist builders. This row of iconic 'Painted Ladies' was built by the developer Matthew Kavanaugh in the San Francisco 'Queen Anne' style, noted for its use of asymmetry, pointed roofs, crenellated detailing and bay windows. Its wooden structure allows a variety of internal layouts based on a standard plan, although the rooms are often small and discrete. The use of the innovative and flexible balloon-frame construction is particularly suited to this location, prone, as it is, to tremors and earthquakes.

'Painted Ladies', San Francisco, CA, 1894–5. **Matthew Kavanaugh**. Active USA, late nineteenth century.

Tipi Blackfoot

Originally an agrarian people, the Blackfoot adapted quickly to the imported culture of guns, which revolutionized buffalo hunting. The tipi, meaning 'dwelling', afforded them absolute freedom of movement, which was vital on the Northern Plains in order to hunt the migratory buffalo. Its conical structure was formed by placing four foundation poles into the ground, then lashing about twenty poles together at the apex and covering it with buffalo hides held down with stones and pegs. An interior skin was used for insulation and waterproofing. Inside, a hide curtain formed an ante-chamber to separate the children from their parents. While they had earned a reputation for bellicosity, the Blackfoot were, conversely, among the most highly skilled of the Native American artists. Dreams, visions and symbolic representations of their cosmology of three parallel universes, as well as colourful scenes of animals or skies cast with thunder, embellished the exterior of their tipis.

Tipi, Northern Plains, MT, c1900. **Blackfoot**. Active USA, sixteenth century onwards.

Bailey House Irving Gill & Frank Mead

Sitting high above the ocean in La Jolla, California, this curious house appears out of place in the stark landscape of the rock cliffs. Designed by Irving Gill in 1907 during a short-lived partnership with Frank Mead, an American who had recently returned from North Africa, the house combines an eclectic mix of Arts and Crafts detailing, popular Spanish Mission motifs and Moorish features. At the request of the client, who was from the Midwest, this weekend home was designed to resemble a barn with a large, double-height living room and an open balcony hallway leading to the upstairs bedrooms. Gill was trained in the Chicago office of Louis Sullivan, along with the young Frank Lloyd Wright, before setting up his own practice in 1893. His progressive politics, his fight to improve building standards, and his pioneering use of cubic forms and architectural concrete have earned him a reputation as one of the unsung heroes of early American Modernism.

Gamble House Greene & Greene

One of the Greene brothers' 'ultimate bungalows', the Gamble House exhibits the plaited nature and superb craftsmanship of their aesthetic: an interweaving of textures, of timber shingles, clinker brick and wooden battening. The layered nature of this construction is also reflective of an interweaving of traditions: Gustav Stickley and the American Arts and Crafts movement, and the Japanese tradition of wooden construction were both absorbed by the Greenes and seamlessly synthesized in a vernacular regionalist idiom shared by such other California architects as Bernard Maybeck and Julia Morgan. The house is less open on the interior than Frank Lloyd Wright's Prairie Houses, but makes extensive use of verandas and balconies to exploit the views over a riverbed and distant mountains. The rich interiors of mahogany and teakwood exude a sense of ease suitable to the relaxed, idyllic lifestyle of Pasadena at the turn of the century.

Gamble House, Pasadena, CA, 1907–9. **Charles Sumner Greene**. b Brighton, OH, 1868. d Carmel, CA, 1957. **Henry Mather Greene**. b Brighton, OH, 1870. d Pasadena, CA, 1954.

Roos House Bernard Maybeck

Designed by the architect of the Piranesian, Neo-Classical Palace of Fine Arts in San Francisco, the Roos House takes on a more medieval character. A facade of ornamental, half-timber framework of redwood, infilled with white-painted stucco, supports quatrefoil tracery, reflecting Bernard Maybeck's early experience in furniture design and adding an overall sense of whimsy to the house. That which appears ornamental on the exterior becomes structural on the interior, with the heavy redwood beams demonstrably supporting the double-storey living room in the manner of an Art and Crafts manor house. The house has an innovative raft-like foundation, which permits the structure to rock with the movement of the earth during quakes and eliminates the need for heavy foundation walls. The overall composition of the Roos House is, at once, whimsical and baronial, setting the tone for the informal fantasy of Bay Area styles to come.

Roos House, San Francisco, CA, 1909. **Bernard Maybeck**. **b** New York, NY, 1862. **d** San Francisco, CA, 1957.

Bradley House Louis Sullivan

One of the most influential forces of the Chicago School and mentor to the young Frank Lloyd Wright, Louis Sullivan designed some of the finest houses in turn-of-the-century North America. In the Bradley House, his most complex and mature domestic work, Sullivan employed a cross-shaped plan using the heavy-walled entry vestibule as the symbolic heart of the house. From this space, the two axes radiate out into a sequence of rooms. On the exterior, the dominant volume containing the main living and sleeping areas is intersected by a smaller block, which is more expressively articulated and features a semi-circular study. Any impression of heaviness is alleviated by cantilevered porches at each end of the building, and long strips of windows down the side elevations. The house is a vibrant example of Sullivan's philosophy that form should follow function; an approach he always inflected with his sensitive employment of Beaux-Arts organic ornamentation.

Bradley House, Madison, WI, 1910. **Louis Henry Sullivan. b** Boston, MA, 1856. **d** Chicago, IL, 1924.

Kykuit Delano & Aldrich

Kykuit has been the home to America's Rockefeller family since 1913, the year it was completed as a country retreat for John D Rockefeller Snr. The architects, Delano & Aldrich, were prominent society architects, trained in the Beaux-Arts tradition. A study in symmetry with its tall, elaborately carved facade, Kykuit, like many American Beaux-Arts buildings, draws architectural inspiration from several European sources, including the Italian Renaissance and the French Norman house. It is situated to overlook magnificent gardens (by landscape architect, William Welles Bosworth) with fountains and stone terraces, as well as to enjoy the panorama of the Hudson River beyond. The gardens and the interiors (designed by Ogden Codman) were influenced by Edith Wharton's book, *Italian Villas and their Gardens*, of 1904. The house today provides a showcase for the Rockefeller collections of ceramics, furniture, paintings and sculpture.

Kykuit, Pocantico Hills, NY, 1913. **William Adams Delano**. b New York, NY, 1874. d New York, NY, 1960. **Chester Holmes Aldrich**. b Providence, RI, 1871. d Rome, Italy, 1940.

30

Frick Residence Carrère & Hastings

With its loggia, refined stonework and the clear delineation of its precinct from the public street, the Frick Residence exudes Neo-Classical grandeur, even though more recent neighbours overshadow it. Carrère & Hastings proved they were able to satisfy American plutocratic taste nearly as well as their more original rivals, McKim Mead & White.

In its prime location on New York's Fifth Avenue, overlooking Central Park, it followed a convention at least a generation old for the very wealthy to live uptown; but domestic arrangements were not Henry Clay Frick's priority. Built towards the end of his life, when he had long been one of America's richest citizens, Frick intended the house

to become a museum after the death of himself and his wife, for his expensive and increasingly refined art collection. The interior, despite its fabulous artworks, is almost as inscrutable as the exterior: part institution, part tomb, part museum — but almost nothing to do with domesticity.

Frick Residence, New York, NY, 1913–14. **John Merven Carrère**. b Rio de Janeiro, Brazil, 1858. d New York, NY, 1911. **Thomas Hastings**. b New York, NY, 1860. d New York, NY, 1929.

Springwood James & Franklin D Roosevelt

Springwood started out as a clapboard farmhouse, was later transformed into a summer house befitting a future American president, and was witness to portentous moments in history and numerous important visitors, among them Winston Churchill and King George VI. The house was originally built in 1826 in the US Federal style

and purchased by James Roosevelt in 1867, who then began what was to be more than three decades of improvements and enlargements that transformed it into the Victorian style. Still later enlargements and adaptions by his wife, Sara, produced the sober, classicized stone and stucco mansion, with its wood-panelled rooms, that

it is today. In 1882, their son, Franklin D Roosevelt, was born at Springwood and lived there throughout his life. In the grounds, his wife Eleanor built her own cottage, Val-Kil, and in 1938, Roosevelt continued the family tradition and commissioned work for a presidential library.

Springwood, Hyde Park, NY, 1826–1915. **James Roosevelt. b** USA, 1828. **d** USA, 1900. **Franklin Delano Roosevelt. b** Hyde Park, NY, 1882. **d** Warm Springs, GA, 1942.

Vizcaya Francis B Hoffman Jr & Paul Chalfin

Vizcaya is a palazzo built, not in the Veneto, but in Miami on the shore of Biscayne Bay. Its owner, James Deering, was an heir to a Midwestern American farm equipment fortune who, having travelled widely, chose to retire to the comparatively untamed subtropical wilderness that was Miami in the early twentieth century. He purchased 180 acres and his interior designer, Paul Chalfin, hired the young architect Francis Burrall Hoffman to design a house. Hoffman was constricted in his choice of form, given Chalfin's proposed re-creations of Italian Renaissance interiors, often using original wall elements and treasures shipped over from Europe. Designed around a palazzo-style courtyard (unfortunately enclosed in the 1980s with a dark pyramid roof), the house became a virtual museum of the decorative arts. There are also Italian gardens designed by Diego Suarez, a quaint 'farm village', and just offshore, a stone barge designed by Sterling Calder.

Vizcaya, Miami, FL, 1914–17. **Francis Burrall Hoffman Jr. b** New Orleans, LA, 1882. **d** Hobe Sound, FL, 1980. **Paul Chalfin. b** USA, 1873. **d** USA, 1959.

Kings Road Studios Rudolph Schindler

The soothing palette of this experimental house reflected the independent lifestyle chosen by its adventurous inhabitants. Designed by Rudolph Schindler for himself, his wife and another couple, this unusual architectural composition consisted of four individual studios and a shared kitchen. Arranged in pairs, each L-shaped set of studios framed a private outdoor patio with a fireplace that served as a traditional living room in the warm climate of southern California. The couples slept on the roof in open-air sleeping lofts and ate food grown in their own garden. A student of Otto Wagner's in Vienna, Schindler began working for Frank Lloyd Wright in Chicago in 1917.

While in California on a project, he became captivated with the warm climate, lifestyle and the many opportunities he found there, so he and his wife settled in Los Angeles. They sponsored fellow Austrian architect, Richard Neutra, to join them, and their families shared the Kings Road Studios from 1925 to 1928.

Kings Road Studios, Los Angeles, CA, 1921–2. **Rudolph Michael Schindler**. b Vienna, Austria, 1887. d Los Angeles, CA, 1953.

Casa Nana Addison Mizner

Sprawling and grand, the Casa Nana — the last of Addison Mizner's large-scale Palm Beach houses — was designed for a Danish immigrant whose fortunes came from a chain of Midwestern American grocery stores. Mizner, a Californian, arrived at Palm Beach at the end of World War I and quickly became the innovator of an architectural style that would become synonymous with Palm Beach. His form of Mediterranean Revival architecture drew on Moorish, Spanish, French, Italian Renaissance, Venetian and Central American sources combined to create an evocative 'old world' atmosphere. The focal element of this house is a rounded stair tower which has an open arcade that paces the spiralling rise of the stairs. The tower not only provides ascent, but is also the main entrance to the house. The fact that it was separate to the house itself gave rise to the legend that Mizner had forgotten to include it, although that was not the case.

Casa Nana, Palm Beach, FL, 1926. **Addison Mizner. b** Benicia, CA, 1872. **d** Palm Beach, FL, 1933.

Aluminaire House Lawrence Kocher & Albert Frey

Built for the Allied Arts and Building Products Exhibition in New York, the all-metal Aluminaire House was a pioneering structure when erected, in only ten days, in 1931. It was the first steel and aluminium house built in the United States, and one of the earliest examples of the budding International Style. The affordable, lightweight, three-storey house followed the development of the experimental prefabricated houses of Le Corbusier, who proposed the Dom-Ino House in 1914, and Buckminster Fuller's Dymaxion House in 1927. The client, architect Wallace K Harrison, purchased the Aluminaire House as a summer retreat and moved it from its original site to two further locations on Long Island, as if to demonstrate its adaptability. Preservationists fought successfully to save the ageing structure and secure it as an historic landmark. The New York Institute of Technology later purchased it and restored the structure to its original metallic glory.

Aluminaire House, Syosset, NY, 1931. **Lawrence Kocher**. b San Jose, CA, 1885. d Williamsburg, VA, 1969. **Albert Frey**. b Zurich, Switzerland, 1904. d Palm Springs, CA, 1998.

Lescaze House William Lescaze

The facade of this radically remodelled brownstone house appears to be a white frame with large areas of glazing, rather than a stone wall with windows punched into it. Swiss-born and trained William Lescaze sought to reverse every convention of his neighbours' houses. Built just after Henry-Russell Hitchcock and Philip Johnson had sanitized

Modernism for American consumption as the 'International Style', this house remains one of its finest examples in New York. A discreet ground-level entrance leads to the studio (brownstone entrances tend to be slightly below street level), while the living quarters are above, reached via a flight of steps under the cantilevered canopy.

Internally, Lescaze created a remarkable series of spaces in the long, thin site, creatively using rooflights, lightwells and terraces, and culminating in a roof-garden. With this, his own house and studio, he demonstrated that modern living was compatible with existing urban form.

Lescaze House, New York, NY, 1934. **William Lescaze**. b Geneva, Switzerland, 1896. d New York, NY, 1969.

Fallingwater Frank Lloyd Wright

With its dramatic, horizontal concrete slabs cantilevered over the roaring crescendo of a waterfall, Fallingwater symbolizes both the romance of nature and the triumph of man. At first glance, the horizontal emphasis is reminiscent of the prevalent International Modernism of the time; however, the natural materials and hand-crafted details — evident in the stacked stone walls — betray its roots in the Arts and Crafts tradition, while the plan is derived from Frank Lloyd Wright's earlier Prairie House-type, with volumes developing from a central core. The contrast between man and nature continues on the inside: the polished flagstone floor appears as though a river had flowed over it for centuries, yet the recessed ceilings float overhead as man-made works of art. Arguably the most important twentieth-century house in the United States, Fallingwater was built towards the latter part of Wright's extraordinarily prolific and influential career.

Fallingwater (Kaufmann House), Bear Run, PA, 1935–9. **Frank Lloyd Wright**. **b** Richland Center, WI, 1867. **d** Phoenix, AZ, 1959.

Wichita House Richard Buckminster Fuller

This circular, aluminium, single-unit dwelling was a prototype for a mass-producible, lightweight house with pre-moulded, pre-installed services, capable of being transported and erected anywhere. It built on Buckminster Fuller's visionary ideas first explored in his 1927 Dymaxion House project (dynamic plus maximum efficiency), which was technologically ahead of its time. The floors were to be laid on pneumatic bladders, suspended by tensile cables from a central mast anchored in a solid base which contained septic and fuel tanks. The external walls were to be of transparent plastic with curtains of aluminium sheeting, and the doors operated by photo-electric cells.

Fuller was editor of the environmental magazine, *Shelter*, in the 1930s, and it was his commitment to industrialization of the building process as the key to 'solving total humanity's evolutionary shelter problems' while respecting the earth's resources, that underpinned his designs.

Wichita House, KS, 1946. **Richard Buckminster Fuller**. **b** Milton, MA, 1895. **d** Los Angeles, CA, 1983.

Hearst Castle Julia Morgan

'La Cuesta Encantada', the Enchanted Hill, was how William Randolph Hearst described this audacious retreat he had built overlooking the Pacific Ocean. Resembling a flamboyant Spanish mission church, the castle appears to be designed as a stage-set for the Hollywood stars who were among Hearst's frequent guests. Built over twenty years, the complex grew to 130 rooms, with decorative elements and artworks drawn mainly from southern Europe and inserted into a reinforced concrete structure. Besides the main house, there are guest cottages, outdoor and indoor pools, greenhouses, a zoo and a pergola encircling the hill for over a mile. Tycoon Hearst was the inspiration for the movie *Citizen Kane*, and his castle, in turn, a model for Kane's fictional house, Xanadu. Trained at the École des Beaux-Arts in Paris (the first woman to be admitted), Julia Morgan's knowledge of Classical architecture and engineering enabled her to supervise every aspect of this enormous project.

Hearst Castle, San Simeon, CA, 1919–47. **Julia Morgan**. b San Francisco, CA, 1872. d San Francisco, CA, 1957.

Airstream Trailer Airstream Co.

Dubbed 'Airstream' because the trailer rode the highways as smoothly as a stream of air, the 1947 model shown in this promotional photograph moves along under the cycling power of French racing champion, Monsieur Latourneau. The picture was later stylized to serve as a logo for the company, to suggest more graphically that the aluminium-clad 'land yacht' — first launched in 1936 by Wally Byam as the Airstream Clipper — was (and still is) strategically designed to be light, manoeuvrable and sturdy. A fully and artfully equipped home, it accommodates comfortable living on and off the road. Following Byam's creed to limit exterior changes to the functional rather than the fashionable, today's Airstream is still highly recognizable and its now iconic streamlined profile and aircraft-like construction have been attracting owners for seven decades. Thousands of vintage Airstreams are still seen at caravan rallies, on movie sets or in museums.

Airstream Trailer, USA, 1947. **Airstream Co**. Established Los Angeles, CA, 1932, now in Jackson Center, OH. **Wally Byam**. b Baker, OR, 1896. d CA, 1962.

Kaufmann Desert House Richard Neutra

Designed as a pavilion for inhabiting and encountering the arid desert of Palm Springs, the Kaufmann Desert House radiates out from its centre like a pin-wheel, with each wing only one room wide in order to maximize the views of the surrounding mountains and landscape. The house sensitively adapts the International Style to this hot, harsh climate, using strong horizontal lines to contrast with the mountainous landscape. Working in the California regionalist tradition of Rudolph Schindler, Neutra combines a Modernist vocabulary with a distinctive American accent, evocative of Frank Lloyd Wright's Taliesin West. Here, however, the steel-frame house retains an intrusive presence, unlike Wright's organicism. The house fulfils Neutra's aspiration that his architecture achieve 'the goal of building environmental harmony, functional efficiency, and human enhancement into the experience of everyday living'.

Kaufmann Desert House, Palm Springs, CA, 1946–7. **Richard Josef Neutra. b** Vienna, Austria, 1892. **d** Wuppertal, Germany, 1970.

Breuer House II Marcel Breuer

The controlled simplicity of this Breuer house — essentially two rectangular forms, one of natural timber cantilevered over another of white-washed concrete — demonstrates his direct and rational design method. Such a disarmingly simple organization, stemming from a very straightforward idea, is characteristic of both Breuer's architecture and his furniture designs, such as his famous tubular chrome and black leather Wassily armchair (1925) from his time at the Bauhaus school. Built into a hillside, this house is relatively small but very open, with large banks of windows and an overhanging balcony suspended by thin, steel cables; a workshop is contained within the concrete base.

His attention to detail, as in the diagonal boarding of the cantilevered portions of the house, helps to define the importance of each element. Breuer's iconic housing designs have often been used as prototypes for practical solutions to domestic design.

Breuer House II, New Canaan, CT, 1947–8. **Marcel Breuer**. b Pécs, Hungary, 1902. d New York, NY, 1981.

Eames House Charles & Ray Eames

Lightweight, steel-and-glass, and in the perpetual sunshine of southern California, the Eames House presented an enticing image to other architects, but especially to British architects: Norman Foster, Richard Rogers, John Winter and Michael Hopkins have all paid tribute to it. If one building launched British 'High Tech', this is it. The husband and wife team responded to the Case Study House Program, initiated by the magazine *Arts & Architecture*, to demonstrate the applicability of modern design to domestic buildings. The house and its associated studio (visible beyond the house) create as much space as possible with minimal materials. Developing an identifiable aesthetic out of such practical construction gave it an enduring place in the canon of great architectural works. Elevating the ordinary, the everyday and 'found objects' became the Eames's hallmark, particularly in the eclectic mix of artfully ordered objects inside the house.

Eames House (Case Study House No.8), Pacific Palisades, CA, 1949. **Charles Eames**. b St Louis, MS, 1907. d St Louis, MS, 1978. **Ray Eames**. b Sacramento, CA, 1912. d Los Angeles, CA, 1988.

Hollin Hills Charles Goodman

Transparent and light, this flat-roofed and purposely simple prefabricated house was part of a grand experiment to provide efficient and economical housing. Begun in 1949, Hollin Hills was one of America's first post-war 'modern' communities and became a laboratory for Charles Goodman's experiments in prefabrication. Over the course of a little more than two decades, 458 homes were built in this wooded suburb outside of Washington, DC. Goodman went on to work as a consulting architect to the National Homes Corporation, a manufacturer of prefabricated houses, where at least 100,000 of his houses were produced. His work involved experimenting with new materials, such as aluminium, in an attempt to create light, open houses. A wall, he wrote, is 'a series of parts joined together … the opaque element and the transparent element which allows you to have privacy where you want it and openness where you want it.'

Hollin Hills, Fairfax County, VA, begun 1949. **Charles Goodman**. b USA, 1906. d USA, 1992.

Dome House Paolo Soleri

Imagine sleeping comfortably under the stars in the Arizona desert, free to gaze at a 360-degree view of the sky. This was the challenge for Paolo Soleri and Mark Mills when they were asked to build a home for Nora Woods on a site near Phoenix, in 1949. The dwelling is composed of two contrasting parts: a solid masonry base carved into the hillside, containing a studio and the cool sleeping quarters for the hot summer months, and the transparent, light-filled main living area, shown here. The rotating glass dome is constructed of two intersecting half-domes, one transparent and the other aluminium-painted to reflect the heat. A copper tube sprays water along its base as a further defence against the desert heat. Since building the Dome House, Soleri's continued interest in an ecologically responsive architecture and lifestyle led to his most ambitious project, an experimental prototype community in Arizona called Arcosanti, which he has been building since 1970.

Dome House, Cave Creek, AZ, 1949. **Paolo Soleri**. b Turin, Italy, 1919.

Glass House Philip Johnson

This structure, small in scale yet prodigious in terms of its influence, shows Philip Johnson's indebtedness to the work of Mies van der Rohe — in the use of standard steel sections for a strong yet decorative finish of the facade, in the corner treatment and the relation of the column to the 1945 sketches for the as yet unbuilt Farnsworth House —

and is an iconic work in the International Style. But Johnson is working here almost as a landscape designer, treating the house as a frame for its natural environment; he uses the lawn, extended on to the raised platform, as a well-groomed carpet on which to place the architectural object. The house is externally symmetrical, and organized

around an interior brick cylinder, which stands in contrast to the incorporeality of the glass envelope. The French architect, Auguste Perret, on visiting the house reportedly remarked, 'Trop de verre' (Too much glass).

Glass House, New Canaan, CT, 1949. **Philip Cortelyon Johnson**. b Cleveland, OH, 1906. d New Canaan, CT, 2005.

Case Study House Raphael Soriano

Blurring the boundaries between interior and exterior, this austere California home was an experiment in residential, light steel-frame construction, and marked Raphael Soriano's shift from Bauhaus white cubes to more informal structures. Designed for the Case Study House Program — sponsored by *Arts & Architecture* magazine to showcase the work of young architects — all of the structural building components were prefabricated and assembled on site in three days. Soriano delighted in working with off-the-shelf materials, such as plywood partitions and window panels that fitted into a standardized grid system, the fundamental ordering principle behind all his work. By leaving portions of the roof grid open, he created interior patios and allowed light to penetrate unexpectedly into the living spaces. Soriano began his career in the office of Richard Neutra, whose Lovell House (1927–9) was an early example of domestic steel construction.

1950 Case Study House, Pacific Palisades, CA, 1950. **Raphael Soriano**. b Rhodes, Greece, 1907. d Los Angeles, CA, 1988.

48

Farnsworth House Ludwig Mies van der Rohe

The view of the Farnsworth House through the trees is one of the supreme delights of Modern architecture. The most exquisite of the glass-box houses, it hangs from a steel frame, its travertine floor suspended well above ground level, which is liable to heavy (sometimes devastating) flooding from the nearby Fox River. Designed as the perfect weekend retreat, it is a single volume completely open to view, with an elegant, timber-veneered service core enclosing a fireplace on one side, kitchen and services on the other, and a bathroom at each end. Its open entrance porch occupies one-third of the entire floor space. As the ultimate example of International Style minimalism applied to domestic living, it has been much debated — not least by the client whose relationship with Mies deteriorated into legal action as the estimated price rocketed. The house has been widely quoted and inspired Philip Johnson's Glass House.

Farnsworth House, Plano, IL, 1946–50. **Ludwig Mies van der Rohe (Ludwig Mies)**. b Aachen, Germany, 1886. d Chicago, IL, 1969.

Eichler Home Joseph Eichler

This typical Eichler Home turns its back on the street and focuses all of its attention on the ample leisure area in the private back yard. Well-designed, inexpensive modern homes were hard to find in the San Francisco Bay area before businessman-turned-building contractor Joseph Eichler built his first housing development in 1950. While living in a rented Frank Lloyd Wright house, Eichler conceived of a new breed of affordable housing that would not sacrifice quality for cost. Although modest in scale, Eichler Homes have impressive features, such as open floor plans, high ceilings, exposed redwood beams and underfloor heating. Bedrooms and bathrooms are often on the street side to reinforce the private nature of the main living space. The characteristic rear glass facades create continuous views overlooking the yard and remain one of the most popular features of the homes. Today, 11,000 Eichler Homes still survive in the San Francisco Bay area.

Eichler Home, various locations, San Francisco Bay area, CA, as built 1950s and 60s. **Joseph Eichler**. b New York, NY, 1900. d San Francisco, CA, 1974.

Goldman House Joseph Esherick

Joseph Esherick, whose work has been termed Bay Region Style, made a conscious effort to depart from the white Modernism of his contemporaries to design houses that reflected more directly his clients' needs, the site, the climate and the historical urban context. The Goldman House, with its environmentally conscious, L-shaped plan enclosing a shady east-facing garden, avoids the more common approach used in the Bay area, where the glazing is exposed to the elements. With this basic arrangement in place, Esherick employed natural daylight to modulate the internal environmental conditions throughout the high-ceilinged, sometimes double-height spaces. The glazing is broken up with a grid of mullions, making reference to the many Victorian houses in the San Francisco Bay area. The Goldman House exemplifies Esherick's rejection of formal concepts of purity and embraces humanity, nature and a Californian architectural tradition.

Goldman House, San Francisco, CA, 1951. **Joseph Esherick. b** Philadelphia, PA, 1914. **d** San Francisco, CA, 1998.

Umbrella House Paul Rudolph

Paul Rudolph believed that an aesthetically unified form could be created only by the successful realization of its function, as seen in his Umbrella House, its distinctive characteristics due to his response to the Lido Shores site. Sheltering from the subtropical sun under a timber canopy, this home is a structurally independent glass and steel box,

yet the 'umbrella', house, pool and terrace form one unit. Glass walls, open floor plan and double-height living space accentuate the interdependence of internal and external volumes. Jalousies set into the north and south walls provide ventilation and shade. Inspired by Gropius's design philosophy while at Harvard, Rudolph endeavoured to

'build meaningfully', focusing on qualities such as simplicity, use of light and shadow, and continuity of space. A major figure of the Sarasota School of Architecture (a post-war Florida style), he developed a new expression for American modernism that was influenced by the Brutalist aesthetic, which is most evident in his civic architecture.

Umbrella House, Lido Shores, Sarasota, FL, 1953. **Paul Rudolph**. b Elkton, KY, 1918. d New York, NY, 1997.

Bavinger House Bruce Goff

'The most gaped-at new house in the US,' said *Life* magazine of the Bavinger House, one of an extraordinary series of experimental houses designed by Bruce Goff. The house was self-built by the sculptor-client, Bavinger, with his family and his students. Sited on a small, rocky ravine — the bridge helps stabilize the house — a single mast, made of two oil-drilling pipes and old biplane wires, supports a copper-covered timber roof over a single, continuous spiral space. The kitchen and bathroom are tucked into the core of the spiral. Protruding into the main space are a series of open pods, used for dining or sleeping and upholstered top and bottom, with separating curtains and netting. A rubble-stone wall wraps around this form, rising from 2 m to 15 m (6 ft to 50 ft) at the centre. While Goff's work had moved on from his early influences by Frank Lloyd Wright, he continued to develop the use of site, materials and programme as key elements.

Bavinger House, Norman, OK, 1950–5. **Bruce Goff**. **b** Alton, KS, 1904. **d** Tyler, TX, 1982.

J Irwin & Xenia Miller House Eero Saarinen

Eero Saarinen, the son of Finnish architect, Eliel Saarinen, already had a longtime familial connection with J Irwin Miller when he was asked to design this house on the Flatrock River in Columbus. This classically modern house is actually four separate structures arranged into one unit under a skylighted metal roof and has been likened to a modern version of Palladio's Villa Rotunda. On the interior, Saarinen used marble for walls and travertine for the floor, which extends out onto an all-round veranda; the furnishings included rugs and chairs that Saarinen designed himself. The Millers commissioned two of only four built single-family residences by Saarinen, who is better known for his more famous public buildings, such as the TWA terminal at Kennedy Airport (1956–62) with its wing-like vaulting roofs. In this building, he used form in an abstract and highly symbolic manner quite different to the contained and geometric form of the Miller House.

J Irwin & Xenia Miller House, Columbus, IN, 1953–7. **Eero Saarinen**. **b** Kirkkonummi, Finland, 1910. **d** Ann Arbor, MI, 1961.

Stahl House Pierre Koenig

'Los Angeles is their back yard' was the way the *Los Angeles Examiner* described the new house of the Stahls in 1960. Pierre Koenig's second house for John Entenza's Case Study House Program is the epitome of the reductivist architecture of the 'Contemporary' style of 1950s California. With its welded steel frame and roof deck, overhanging eaves and open-air swimming pool, it still features regularly in many fashion and film shoots. Built on a relatively cheap site, due to its poor soil and steeply sloping aspect, the owners wanted to take full advantage of the impressive view. Koenig cantilevered the main living space of the steel-frame house out over the slope on massive reinforced concrete beams supported by huge caissons bored into the ground. In 1989, a Case Study exhibition, 'Blueprints for Modern Living', produced a full-scale mock-up of the house, using television screens to represent the lights of the city below.

Stahl House (Case Study House No.22), Los Angeles, CA, 1960. **Pierre Koenig**. b San Francisco, CA, 1925. d Los Angeles, CA, 2004.

Esherick House Louis Kahn

In this building, Louis Kahn endowed what is, in effect, a small suburban house — constructed in the stuccoed, timber-frame vernacular of countless such houses — with something of the monumentality of ancient architecture. He achieved this using two means. First, a plan of almost Palladian simplicity: two long, deep rooms either side of a staircase hall, one side a double-height living room, the other a dining room with a bedroom above it, and a service block to the side. Second, the facades onto the street and garden have deep alcoves — solid with bookshelves on the street side, and largely open on the garden side. Solid timber doors to the garden, set back the whole depth of the reveal, alternate with wider bays of glazing set flush to the outer face of the wall, forming full-height bay windows. In his later public buildings, Kahn would achieve a greater monumentality using more solid materials, but even in this modest house, the grandeur of his aim remains impressive.

Esherick House, Chestnut Hill, PA, 1959–61. **Louis Isadore Kahn**. b Saaremaa, Estonia, 1901. d New York, NY, 1974.

Greene Residence Herb Greene

Herb Greene based the form of his house on that of the American buffalo, which used to roam the prairies of the Midwest in great numbers. He tried to inject a feeling of pathos into the 'looming, wounded creature' that is the house; but it also evokes a natural shelter, with the entrance under a metaphorical spreading wing, like that of a mother hen. There is a strong sense of accretion and collage, an organic gathering of form and materials to create a strong physical presence. Inside, the house is cave-like, the irregularly layered wooden shingles creating comforting texture and rhythms; while the relation of the different levels and the expression of the exterior form internally are simultaneously dramatic and vertiginous. Herb Greene was one of the most talented architects to study under Bruce Goff, whose eclectic expressionistic style has clearly influenced Greene's work, as well as his humanistic approach to organic architecture, expressive of life and feeling.

Greene Residence (Prairie Chicken House), Norman, OK, 1961. **Herb Greene.** b New York, NY, 1929.

Moore House Charles Moore

One of the most prolific and influential architectural practitioners, writers and teachers of his time, Charles Moore invested the many houses he designed for himself with his original, and often whimsical artistry. Despite tight budget constraints, this small house near San Francisco — one of his early projects — displays all the artistic invention for which Moore became renowned. Two groups of massive, solid timber Tuscan columns form the dramatic primary structure and planning nucleus of the house. Above each cluster (one defining the living space, the other a sunken bath), a white-painted pyramidal skylight floods the interior with daylight. The juxtaposition between the heavy structure and the lightweight external envelope is emphasized by the fact that the walls never meet at the corners, where you would expect to find structural support. Instead, sliding glass panels open the building up to views of the oak forest beyond.

Vanna Venturi House Robert Venturi

The flat, overstated, metaphorical facade of this house has become an icon of late twentieth-century Post-Modern domestic architecture. Robert Venturi designed this house — his first built work — for his mother while he was still young. She had asked for comparative simplicity, yet did not want a modern house that would be incompatible with her antique furniture. This now-famous facade makes reference to Classical architecture, but does so using overscaled elements. It has a skewed symmetry and is primarily an oversized gable with a chimney set slightly off-centre, rising above it. The interior offers a similar mix; it fulfils familiar domestic expectations, while at the same time important elements, such as the fireplace and chimney, have a competitive rather than compatible relationship. Venturi refined his notions of complexity and contradiction over the years in increasingly large projects, not least the National Gallery extension in London (1991).

Vanna Venturi House (Mother's House), Chestnut Hill, PA, 1959–64. **Robert Charles Venturi**. **b** Philadelphia, PA, 1925.

Gwathmey House and Studio Charles Gwathmey

Set in a former potato field, this house and artist's studio were intended to appear sculpted, as though carved out of a solid block of wood. Charles Gwathmey, a leading Modernist and one of the New York Five, began work on the larger of the two structures — the house itself (in the foreground) — in 1965, and completed the studio in 1967.

The clients were his parents, a painter and a photographer, who commissioned their son just after he left his apprenticeship with Edward Larrabee Barnes. The interiors echo the geometries of the exterior: a workroom and guest bedrooms on the ground floor, and an external staircase leading up to a double-height living room on the first floor,

with kitchen and dining areas. The studio block is positioned at an angle to the main house; the design intent was to create a sense of movement between the two. Gwathmey later went on to design the addition to a great, sculptural masterpiece, Frank Lloyd Wright's Guggenheim Museum, which was completed in 1992.

Gwathmey House and Studio, Amagansett, NY, 1965–7. **Charles Gwathmey**. **b** Charlotte, NC, 1938.

Drop City Droppers

In 1965, three artists bought land in southern Colorado and started what was to become one of the most famous (some say infamous) group communities of the 1960s. The Droppers — writers, painters, musicians and film-makers who made up the community — were determined to live free, creative lives outside the bounds of established society. They based the design of their distinctive shelters on polyhedral geometry using inexpensive locally available materials such as plywood, chickenwire, tarpaper, chopped up car bodies and windscreens. Each dome-shaped structure contained a separate function — the central cluster of domes, seen here, housed bathrooms and the kitchen, while peripheral domes were used as bedrooms, artists' studios and even a mixed-media theatre (seen here on the far left). Not surprisingly, the anti-establishment lifestyle of the Droppers attracted attention, and Drop City became an influential prototype for other co-operative communities.

Drop City, nr Trinidad, CO, 1965–70. **Droppers**. Founded by **Gene Bernofsky**. **b** New York, NY, 1941. **JoAnn Bernofsky**. **b** New York, NY, 1942. **Clark Richert**. **b** Wichita, KS, 1941.

Frank House Peter Eisenman

Peter Eisenman's iconic and elaborate Frank House is one of a sequence of highly theoretical, built experiments of new architectural forms that question the nature and use of family homes. This is achieved by twisting and manipulating the structural grid on which Modernist houses were based. The architectural games affect the occupants' use of the house itself: the marital bed is split down the middle by a slot which cuts through wall, roof and floor — treating the gap as though it were a solid object. Elsewhere in the house, two staircases seem to mirror each other, but one of them is only an illusion — an unusable, red-carpeted form in the ceiling that leads nowhere, making the house appear upside down and challenging the viewer's concept of gravity. Eisenman remains the most formally complex of the New York Five, a group of American architects who experimented with and reinvented strict Modernist forms and beliefs before going their different ways.

Frank House (House VI), West Cornwall, CT, 1972. **Peter Eisenman**. b Newark, NJ, 1932.

Douglas House Richard Meier

Douglas House is situated, almost precipitously, high above Lake Michigan on a steeply sloping site. Richard Meier designed this house early in his career, at a time when his ideas of form and colour (or the absence of colour, Meier's trademark), were drawn largely from his study of the purist work of Le Corbusier. Here, against the background of blue of the lake and sky and the green of the trees, Meier sought a 'dramatic dialogue' that would offer a contrast between the natural and the man-made, enhanced by the vivid whiteness of the house. Entered at roof level via a walkway, the house is arranged so that the lakeside view opens up as one descends to the living and dining areas, with the private spaces facing away from the lake. One of the New York Five group of architects, Meier's strength is in his consistency of an architectural philosophy, demonstrated in his early houses as well as his later public buildings, such as the Getty Museum in Los Angeles (1997).

Douglas House, Harbor Springs, MI, 1971–3. **Richard Meier**. b Newark, NJ, 1934.

Driftwood Tree Huts Earl Harvey

When his son died in a boating accident in 1971, Earl Harvey built these two structures, perched in the top of two redwood trees, as a memorial. Constructed over a period of four years, the timber was salvaged from driftwood and the limbs of lumbered redwoods. The two huts are fixed precariously in the live, forked tree trunks, the leafy branches pushing up beneath giving them the appearance of having sprouted spontaneously from the trees themselves. The huts are accessed (mostly by local children) via a winding stair supported on steel reinforcing bars hammered into the tree trunk. One hut contains a fully-functioning wood-burning stove, while the other houses a more fanciful 'wishing well' — a piece of pipe that winds its way from the floor of the hut to the ground. Dropping coins into a slot in the floor, the children can listen to them rattle their way down to the ground while they make their wish.

Driftwood Tree Huts, Eureka, CA, 1975. **Earl Harvey**. Active USA, mid to late twentieth century.

Daisy House Stanley Tigerman

Perched on a sand dune high above Lake Michigan, this whimsical house challenges the traditional perception of Classical symmetry. Stanley Tigerman conceptualized the design as analogous to the form of the human body, symmetrical on the outside and asymmetrical on the inside. In addition, its plan and elevation refer, subtly, to male and female anatomy. The undulating walls are constructed of vertical cedar boards, accented by an inset doorway and the soft flow of the concrete stairs. Inside, the sleeping quarters are located on either side of the central volume, allowing maximum privacy for children and parents. Post-Modern *enfant terrible* of the Chicago architecture scene since the 1960s, Tigerman is known for his sculptural expression and playful, sometimes controversial approach to design, as demonstrated in particular in his earlier Hot Dog House of 1974.

Daisy House, Porter, IN, 1975. **Stanley Tigerman**. b Chicago, IL, 1930.

Heckscher House Edward Larrabee Barnes

The Heckscher House takes the traditional American Shingle Style and reduces it to the pure simplicity of geometric forms placed gently in the landscape. Edward Larrabee Barnes designed this vacation house to sit delicately amid the spruce trees on a coastal site in Maine. It consists of four separate geometric structures, each recalling traditional vernacular forms without reiterating them, connected by a wooden deck with views to the coastline beyond. An outdoor eating area is shaded, appropriately to its coastal setting, by a sailboat spinnaker set to adjust to the sun's path. As was typical of his work, Barnes — the designer of several important American museums in Dallas and Minneapolis — kept the detailing to a minimum, thus allowing the spaces to have an elegant, abstract simplicity. Barnes was hugely influenced by his teachers, Walter Gropius and Marcel Breuer, after they had left the Bauhaus in Germany to teach at Harvard University.

Heckscher House, Mount Desert Island, ME, 1976. **Edward Larrabee Barnes. b** Chicago, IL, 1915. **d** Cupertino, CA, 2004.

Gehry House Frank Gehry

This view of the entrance to Frank Gehry's own house, on a quiet residential street, demonstrates his attempt to capture the quality of the existing mansard-roofed, asbestos-shingled bungalow within an iconoclastic reconstructed shell, thus celebrating it as an *objet trouvé*. Constructed of fragmented forms made of cheap materials — such as chainlink fencing, plywood and corrugated metal — the house creates a shocking impression with its pierced and skewed forms caught as if in the midst of an earthquake, while acknowledging the iconic quality of the suburban house. Gehry, who won the Pritzker Prize, the lifetime achievement in architecture award, in 1989, was loosely associated with Deconstructivism and Post-Modernism, and went on from this early domestic scale to work on his renowned, large public buildings; in particular, the iconic, steel-clad Guggenheim Museum in Bilbao of 1997.

Gehry House, Santa Monica, CA, 1978. **Frank Owen Gehry**. b Toronto, Canada, 1929.

Pink House Arquitectonica

This is a house of layers, pink upon pink, with gradations from powder-pale to vibrant rose. Designed between 1976 and 1979 by Bernardo Fort-Brescia and Laurinda Spear, the husband-and-wife team behind Arquitectonica, this house grew to define a new era in Miami, ending the long period in which architects spurned the vibrant colours of the tropics. The Pink House is an unconventional Modernist form that draws on the dual traditions of Art Deco and the Bauhaus, both predominant in Miami; its primary building materials are stucco-clad concrete inset with glass blocks. The setting, on the shore of Biscayne Bay, reinforces its tropicality, as does the central feature — a long, narrow internal swimming pool that runs along the entire north–south axis of the building. Founded in 1977, this Miami-based firm has gained an international reputation for its daring use of colour and boldly innovative geometric forms.

Pink House, Miami Shores, FL, 1976–9. **Arquitectonica (ARQ)**. **Bernardo Fort-Brescia**. b Lima, Peru, 1951. **Laurinda Spear**. b Rochester, MN, 1950.

Johnson House Hugh Newell Jacobsen

High up on a hill above the rolling grass of a thousand-acre stud farm is a house that abstracts southern US history and recasts it as modern. Hugh Newell Jacobsen was one of the first to experiment with vernacular forms in an era of straightforward structures, although this house does show a strong Modernist sentiment, and an equally strong penchant for Classicism. The Neo-Classical style was the traditional house form of the South, but this version of the 'house on the hill' suggests the aesthetic without the detail. Like the local architecture, Johnson House is white-painted brick; the columns have travertine at their base and rise to support wooden sunscreens and rafters. White birch trees are planted in the forecourt and echo the grid of the columns. Inside, the single-storey spaces flow into one another, a trademark of Jacobsen's houses, which are often organized as processional experiences while, in this case, still fitting neatly within the constraints of the grid.

Johnson House, Lexington, KY, 1980. **Hugh Newell Jacobsen. b** Grand Rapid, MI, 1929.

Lawson House Robert A M Stern

The Lawson House is a hybrid. Although built in the Shingle Style and scaled as if it were a large and important house, it also draws on the American beach cottage — not the grand cottages of Newport fame, but the simple 'shack by the sea' tradition. Situated on top of a sand dune, the house is approached via an ascending walkway and then a wide, monumentally scaled stairway leading to a shaded porch. The roof is a dominant architectural element, steeply pitched and penetrated by a Roman thermal window. Inside, the living room looks out to sea, while the master bedroom is tucked in the attic under the capacious roof. Robert A M Stern, widely acknowledged as a key theorist and originator of the Post-Modern movement, was influential in reintroducing the Shingle Style and reviving interest in historical American domestic architecture. He describes the Lawson House as a 'marriage of High Classicism with grandma's house'.

Lawson House, East Quogue, Long Island, NY, 1979–81. **Robert A M Stern. b** New York, NY, 1939.

Plocek House Michael Graves

From its sloping wooded site, the Plocek House projects a firm, Classical street-side facade, its three storeys divided into basement, *piano nobile* and attic. The house boasts a grand entrance intended both to reinforce its sense of scale and to imbue it with human proportions. A garden pavilion, set apart from the house, serves as a quiet study.

With its reinterpreted, exaggerated Classicism and muted palette, the Plocek House is the first of Michael Graves's buildings to show this development in his style. Originally influenced by the Modernism of Le Corbusier, Graves became one of the New York Five architects or 'Five Whites', so named for the absence of colour in their work.

Since then, however, he has moved towards designing witty and erudite buildings that have a human scale and exaggerated historical forms. Before the Plocek House, earlier works hinted at Graves's personal vocabulary, but it is with this residence that his distinguished style is revealed.

Plocek House, Warren, NJ, 1982. **Michael Graves**, **b** Indianapolis, IN, 1934.

Boulder House Charles Johnson

The look-out tower of this house rises from enormous, ancient granite boulders that it mimics in shape and texture, blending with the desert in Arizona. Built of stucco-covered masonry, the tower contains the master bedroom suite, located on the upper storey. On the first floor, the glass-enclosed living and dining rooms nestle among the rocks, but open on one side to a terrace with expansive desert views. Charles Johnson roofed the living spaces and tower with vigas (protruding log beams) a building technique that supported the adobe dwellings once common in this region. The main fireplace mantel is covered in plaster, which the architect sculpted by hand to simulate the rustic, curvaceous appearance of adobe walls. The guest room fireplace, under a rock overhang incorporated into the house, was used as a fire pit by native people for many generations. Johnson says, 'I personally call the house "Whispering Boulders", because the rocks had so much to say.'

Boulder House, Carefree, AZ, 1982. **Charles Foreman Johnson**. b Plainfield, NJ, 1929.

Krier House Leon Krier

In a town of towers, this house stands tallest. Leon Krier, a leading proponent of the 1980s New Urbanist movement to return to traditional towns and architecture, was an advisor in the early stages of planning Seaside, the famous new resort community in the Florida Panhandle. He decided to build a house of his own there which has become a landmark in more ways than one. It is a small house on a compact site, but rises high in the air to its 'temple' top that affords a fine view of the Gulf of Mexico. By regulation, all Seaside houses have white picket fences, and this one is no exception. Krier has spent most of his career in the theoretical realm of architecture, writing and drawing, and this house represents his first built work. It is a craftsman's house, intricately assembled as if built by a ship's carpenter. Krier is also known for his planning of the neo-traditional UK town of Poundsbury in Devon, under the instruction of the Prince of Wales.

Krier House, Seaside, FL, 1985 – 7. **Leon Krier**. **b** Echternach, Luxemburg, 1946.

Chmar House Scogin Elam & Bray

As it soars skyward, this house exults in nature while, at the same time, showing deference to it. It is at once a *tour de force* and yet, somehow, quite unassuming. The Chmar House sits on a one-hectare (two-and-three-quarter-acre) site next to a nature preserve; thus the bucolic nature of the setting in the rolling wooded Atlanta countryside, is well protected. The actual placement of the house was selected after a tree fell here, naturally providing a clearing. The house is raised above the ground on tree-like columns to cause as little disruption to nature as possible; the living areas form one wing, and the guest quarters another. The design draws inspiration from Japanese architecture and ritual (the clients are practising Buddhists), so that the spaces unfold as a ceremonial passage. The interiors, clad in birch and plywood panels, with windows of varying shapes and sizes, connect inside once again to nature outside.

Chmar House, Atlanta, GA, 1988 – 9. **Mack Scogin**. b Atlanta, GA, 1943. **Merrill Elam**. b Nashville, TN, 1943. **Lloyd Bray**. b Atlanta, GA, 1951.

Red Cross House Jersey Devil

At the core of this rugged and experimental house in the Florida Keys is a little block-and-stucco cottage, one of dozens erected by the Red Cross in 1935 after a very destructive hurricane swept through Florida. The architects, Jersey Devil — so named as they established their practice in the state of New Jersey — are nomadic, moving from site to site in their Airstream trailer, settling in for the duration of the project's construction. With the cottage as their starting point, they created a complex construction that provides accommodation for family living and work space. Using sturdy, commonplace materials, the building was assembled so as to withstand the sometimes fierce weather — in particular hurricanes. The result is a study in corrugated steel and glass; a house that affords long views out to the ocean and across the Middle Keys from its tower look-out.

Red Cross House, Islamorada, FL, 1991. **Jersey Devil**. **Jim Adamson**. b Ashbury Park, NJ, 1948. **Steve Badanes**. b New York, NY, 1943.

Greenberg House Ricardo Legorreta

The use of the wall as a canvas for the interplay of light and shadow, sun and shade, is emphasized in this house designed by the Mexican architect, Ricardo Legorreta. An heir to the Arab-Hispanic tradition of Luis Barragán, Legorreta utilizes the thickness and variation of massive walls to create a place of privacy and refuge from the outside world. The two towers, one containing a studio, the other a library, contribute to this sense of seclusion. A feeling of calm expansiveness is achieved through the use of a combination of interior atria and exterior terraces; while the desert tones of external ochre-coloured plaster are contrasted on the inside by walls painted in magenta, lavender or cherry. This sculptural style, working in harmony with the desert climate, is a noticeable departure from the steel skeleton and lightweight skin of the modern, domestic California architecture of Rudolph Schindler, Raphael Soriano and Richard Neutra.

Windsor House Duany Plater-Zyberk

The traditions of the Caribbean and Florida's oldest city, St Augustine, inform the architecture of Windsor, a 'new town' on the Florida Atlantic coast. Both the town and this house were designed by Andres Duany and Elizabeth Plater-Zyberk, whose renown has come largely from their pedestrian-orientated town plans as a response to urban sprawl. The architecture of Windsor House relies on such Caribbean-inspired features as broad overhangs, wooden balconies and shutters, breezeways and large windows to permit cross-ventilation — all features of the tropical vernacular. An open loggia connects the main living spaces on the ground floor and, at the same time, borders the swimming pool. Duany Plater-Zyberk is among the leaders of a revived New Urbanist, neo-vernacular architecture in the United States and is also responsible for the planning of the famous New Urbanist resort of Seaside in Florida (1984–91).

Windsor House, Windsor, FL, 1992. **Andres Duany**. b New York, NY, 1949. **Elizabeth Plater-Zyberk**. b Bryn Mawr, PA, 1950.

Stretto House Steven Holl

The pavilions and pools of this house overlap and combine in a rhythm based on a musical score. Holl cites Béla Bartók's *Music for Strings, Percussion and Celeste* as his inspiration; a *stretto* is the close overlapping of two voices or sounds. The architecture takes light and space as its equivalent to the instrumentation and sound in the four movements of the piece. Four concrete dams between three ponds on the site also inform the flowing nature of the house and the subtle progression between different floor levels. These changes in level are also marked by changes in materials and surfaces; while white concrete blocks form the external walls, light curvilinear metal sheeting gently spans the roofs. Holl became known initially for his light-filled and colourful interiors, and his major built works include the critically acclaimed Kiasma, the Museum for Contemporary Art in Helsinki (1998) and the Chapel of St Ignatius, Seattle University, Washington (1997).

Stretto House, Dallas, TX, 1989–92. **Steven Holl**. **b** Bremerton, WA, 1947.

Crawford Residence Morphosis

The diverse mixture of materials and elements of this ocean-view house makes it an 'architecture of fragments'. The house is divided into two components, forcefully split down the centre by a lap pool: one wing for the living, dining and kitchen facilities, and the other for bedrooms. The two are united by a north–south, skylighted 'cosmic' axis on the far side of the house, with only its first storey visible on the street level. Built with the conviction that European Functionalism is unsuited to the unpredictable, chaotic world of southern California, the house expresses Morphosis's contention that the 'Modernist penchant for unification and simplification must be broken'. Headed initially by Thom Mayne and Michael Rotondi (both associated with the inauguration of the rebellious 'SCI-ARC' school of architecture in Los Angeles), the firm sought an architectural pluralism appropriate to its local, cultural and historical setting.

T-House Simon Ungers & Thomas Kinslow

The dominant T-shape of this house contains both residential accommodation and a workspace and library for its owner, a writer who needed space to store his 10,000-volume collection. The two storeys of the bar of the T are divided horizontally into solid and void. The solid top half houses the stacks of books on a mezzanine and the transparent lower half, with views out to the woods, is for working and reading, with direct vertical access to the bookshelves. Visitors enter the house across a promenade deck above the residential part of the house, which is a low-slung pavilion that emerges from the slope of the site. The only external clue to the presence of the lower volume is a funnel-like chimney. The dramatic orange colour of the cladding comes from the effect of the weathering steel shell, which is further dramatized by the regular spacing of black, vertical glazed slots. Without any sense of scale, it is difficult to read.

T-House, Wilton, NY, 1988–92. **Simon Ungers**. b Cologne, Germany, 1957. d 2006. **Thomas Kinslow**. Active USA, late twentieth century.

Lawson-Westen House Eric Owen Moss

The spiralling staircase at the heart of the Lawson-Westen House offers a dramatic moment of architectural abstraction. It is symbolic of the intricacy and disjunction not just of this house, but of much contemporary Californian architecture. The clients for this house said they wanted 'room to breathe', and they had a preference for high-ceilinged living rooms. The architect's interpretation of this brief was to create a split between 'limited and limitless, known and unknown'. The house form is generated by the circular kitchen, which is literally the central hearth where cooking and entertaining take place. Above this, the open staircase has balconies looking back down onto the kitchen and double-height living space, as well as views out through the irregular, strangely shaped windows. With the Lawson-Westen House, Eric Owen Moss has created a house of enormous spatial complexity and unexpected architectural anomalies.

Lawson-Westen House, Brentford, CA, 1988–93. **Eric Owen Moss**. b Los Angeles, CA, 1943.

Turtle Creek House Antoine Predock

The stepped roof of Antoine Predock's Turtle Creek House, resembling the local geology, is designed to be part of the prehistoric trail along a limestone formation, where woodlands, prairie and stream converge. Designed for enthusiastic bird-watchers, the limestone ledges are planted with indigenous vegetation to encourage bird habitats. The network of roof terraces is part of a series of viewing spaces extending across the site, which lie under the major north–south route of migrating birds. The central 'fissure' of the house's rock-like form reveals the entrance foyer, with access to the north wing, containing the main living area, and the south wing, for formal social gatherings; a gallery zone links the wings. Above the entrance, a sky ramp of tensile steel projects into the canopy of trees. Predock's blunt, often windowless architecture is reminiscent of the prevalent adobe house-building traditions of Arizona and New Mexico.

Turtle Creek House, Dallas, TX, 1993. **Antoine Predock**. b Lebanon, MS, 1936.

Golden Beach House Carlos Zapata

The entry facade of this beach-front house, just north of Miami Beach, signals the architect's desire to break the box of Modernism. Sensual materials, such as the translucent wall panels of veined onyx and crisply cut forms, are a radical departure from the 1920s Spanish colonial house — Franklin Roosevelt's former winter retreat — that was demolished to make way for this dramatic ensemble. The new 576 sq m (6,200 sq ft) house sits atop the existing foundations and follows its H-shaped plan almost exactly, with a soaring, double-height entry hall and living space separating the two wings. Its walls, however, take on a whole new life. No two meet at right angles; they are treated as dynamic planes that convey a constant sense of motion and discovery, with suggestive slivers of glass scored into their surface to let in light. Zapata's design recalls the fluid, non-rectilinear designs of contemporaries, such as British-based, Iraqi-born architect, Zaha Hadid.

Drager House Franklin Israel

Built in an area of the Berkeley Hills consumed by fire in 1991, the jagged form of this house expresses an awareness of California as a place of margins rather than centres, split in the middle, like the fault line which runs near to the site. One of Israel's last projects, this house shows his indebtedness to various California building traditions, including the dynamic formal disjunctions of Frank Gehry, the hillside architecture of Richard Neutra, the treatment of the exploded box begun by Rudolph Schindler, as well as a reverence for Japanese architecture as reinterpreted along America's west coast. In addition, Israel draws from the palette and materials of the Arts and Crafts movement, enfolding the house in copper roofing, which spills down its side, replacing the traditional wooden shingles. Attentive to the steep slope of the site, the large corner windows are designed to frame the view.

Drager House, Berkeley Hills, CA, 1994. **Franklin David Israel. b** New York, NY, 1945. **d** Los Angeles, CA, 1996.

House at Shiloh Falls Mockbee Coker

Set on the banks of the Tennessee River, this striking house is the result of an unusual but successful collaboration between client, architect and builder. Built as a weekend retreat for two brothers and their families, the house also accommodates an extensive collection of contemporary photography and pre-Columbian artefacts, requiring it to be part-gallery and part-home. The architects — known as much for their painting and sculpture as for their buildings — worked closely with the builder to elaborate the design and refine the details. Arranged on a linear axis running down the steep site, the house contrasts sharply with the wooded slopes, its angled and irregular geometry jutting through the trees. With its references to local vernacular, including agricultural and industrial motifs in the steel structure and roof, the house embodied the design approach of Mockbee Coker which stressed the importance of making and thinking simultaneously.

House at Shiloh Falls, Hardin County, TN, 1996. **Samuel Mockbee**. b Meridian, MS, 1945. d Jackson, MS, 2001. **Coleman Coker**. b Memphis, TN, 1951.

Ledge House Bohlin Cywinski Jackson

Built on a rocky and forested hillside in the Catoctin Mountains of Maryland, this house derives its name from the man-made ledge on which it has been constructed. It replaces a traditional log cabin that had been built on this ledge in the 1940s, which set the precedent for the form of the building that was to follow. The architects — an American firm known for its work using natural materials — used white cedar logs, heavy Douglas fir timbers, galvanized roofing metal and a quartzite stone brought in from New York's Lake Champlain. This stone, while similar to the local stone, was chosen for its structural and aesthetic superiority. The features of the Ledge House include a massive fireplace constructed of the quartzite, a forecourt which provides an outdoor gathering space and, surprisingly, an indoor pool. The logs and timbers reinforce the concept that the house is an organic part of the forest.

Ledge House, Catoctin Mountains, MD, 1996. **Peter Bohlin**. b Mount Vernon, NY, 1937. **Bernard Cywinski**. b Trenton, NJ, 1940. **Jon Jackson**. b McKees Rocks, PA, 1952.

Nautilus Earthship Michael Reynolds

Michael Reynolds has been building houses from what he describes as 'nuisance resources' for over twenty years and has attracted international attention for his passive solar Earthship buildings. Started in 1994, a development of 130 Earthships, called the 'Greater World Community', is still under construction. One of the houses, overlooking a deep gorge in the rolling mesa, is the Nautilus Earthship. Based on a seashell form, the building is made from discarded car tyres packed with earth and adobe-plastered to form a thermal mass storage heater, absorbing heat during the day and re-radiating it during the night. Rainwater tanks on the roof and photo-voltaic cells on the south facade allow the house to operate independently of mains water and power supplies. Although Reynolds's building forms are unorthodox, they are exemplary in their superior climatic and structural performance and, most importantly, their imaginative use of recyclable resources.

Nautilus Earthship, Taos, NM, 1996. **Michael Reynolds. b** New Albany, IN, 1945.

Sheats House John Lautner

Nearly thirty years after its construction, John Lautner remodelled, or in his own words 'perfected', his original vision for the Sheats House, using modern construction methods. By replacing the 1963 mullions with frameless silicon-sealed glazing, he produced an invisible curtain of air between the living area and its view over the city, which emphasized its almost cave-like quality, a debt to his mentor Frank Lloyd Wright. Lautner was apprenticed to Wright after graduating and became the first of the Taliesin Fellows, before going on to set up his own practice. He revered Wright, although Henry-Russell Hitchcock, the architectural critic, considered that his work could 'stand comparison with that of his master'. It is arguable which of Lautner's houses is the most iconic; but it is indicative that many of them have been featured in films. Others equally celebrated include the Chemosphere residence of 1960 and the Arango House in Acapulco (1977).

Sheats House (Sheats-Goldstein House), Los Angeles, CA, 1963, remodelled 1989–96. **John Lautner**. b Marquette, MI, 1911. d Los Angeles, CA, 1994.

New York City House Tod Williams & Billie Tsien

The transparency of the glazed rear facade of this house in uptown New York contrasts with a more discreet elevation onto the street, in which a large screen of limestone presents a barrier to curious eyes. The building is a rare phenomenon — one of very few new townhouses built in the city in the last half century, replacing two nineteenth-century brownstones on the site. Just as the exterior shows a clear departure from the traditional, the internal layout represents a move away from cellular rooms to a more open, interconnected series of generic spaces. These are filled with daylight entering both laterally and from above, through a large skylight set above a glass-balustraded, five-storey central stairwell. To maximize the available space, the terraced garden is excavated to basement level and accessed via a bridge. The house represents the architects' commitment to the regeneration of the city, to stem the flight of families to suburban areas.

New York City House, New York, NY, 1994–6. **Tod Williams**. **b** Detroit, MI, 1943. **Billie Tsien**. **b** Ithaca, NY, 1949.

Townsend Residence Will Bruder

Previously pseudo-Spanish in style, this house in Arizona was totally remodelled and now reveals itself in a series of five curved, organic volumes. Clad in galvanized metal, aluminium and perforated stainless steel with sandblasted concrete block masonry, the house is illuminated by the desert light as it sits comfortably against its mountainside backdrop, amid extensive desert vegetation. Gallery-like spaces with breathtaking views across Paradise Valley display the owners' collection of contemporary art, crafts and modern furniture. Will Bruder trained as a sculptor before starting his career as an architect under the tutelage of Gunnar Birkerts and Paolo Soleri. Since 1974, he has earned a reputation for architecture that is sensitive to the unusual character of the American desert landscape. His largest project is the Phoenix Central Library of 1995, which opened to widespread acclaim from visitors and the architectural community alike.

Townsend Residence, Paradise Valley, AZ, 1997. **Will Bruder. b** Milwaukee, WI, 1946.

House in West Marin Fernau & Hartman

Situated on a wooded hillside above a lagoon, this house was designed as a complete contrast to compartmentalized urban living. The architects took advantage of the idyllic setting to design a house that would function as a place for three simple activities — eating, playing and resting. The strength of the design lies in the negligible distinction between the interior and the exterior, which is reinforced in every aspect of the house. From the L-shaped courtyard plan that embraces the landscape, to the finely detailed, vertically folding doors that remove even the barrier of glazing, the space extends without limit into its surroundings. Only the road-side elevation has been constructed of solid, environmentally efficient straw-bale to create some degree of privacy. The filtered light of the forest canopy and glimpses of the lagoon beyond become the backdrop to the family's daily activities, unconstrained by the more usual four walls of a city dwelling.

House in West Marin, CA, 1995–9. **Richard Fernau**. **b** Chicago, IL, 1946. **Laura Hartman**. **b** Charlston, WV, 1952.

Zachary House Studio Atkinson

This house in Zachary, Louisiana — the very first project built by Stephen Atkinson — is a variation on a humble housing type common throughout the southern United States, known as the 'dogtrot': two rooms separated by an open breezeway. The house seems almost childlike in its simple profile, rustic corrugated metal exterior and freestanding masonry chimney. However, the typical metal roof of Atkinson's dogtrot is exaggerated by a 45-degree pitch and corrugated metal siding — recalling the exteriors of nearby farm structures — the architect's own embellishments. Corrugated shutters at the ends of the house conceal glazed double doors. The breezeway between the two internal rooms opens onto a long deck extending at a right angle from the house. This home, built for Atkinson's parents in the region where he grew up, shows how powerful even the most modest buildings can be.

Zachary House, Zachary, LA, 1999. **Studio Atkinson. Stephen Atkinson. b** Baton Rouge, LA, 1967.

Hergott Shepard Residence Michael Maltzan Architecture

The street facade of this house appears as a series of opaque volumes that buffer any direct views into the interior, a sense of privacy that is emphasized by a hidden entrance. This external solidity gives way to a system of integrated, transparent spaces behind, some public and others more intimate. At the rear, where the site drops steeply, the house opens onto a terrace with views over Los Angeles. The living space, designed for entertaining and to display the clients' art collection, is split into two double-height interconnecting volumes, which are contained within the diagonally related zinc-clad boxes. A dining area and gymnasium with city views completes the ground floor. The first floor houses a bedroom suite, connected to a study/guest room via an open-air walkway. Maltzan, in keeping with longstanding American attitudes towards private house design, has created an alternative to traditional domestic models that reflects changes in how we live and work, and responds to the needs of the owners' lifestyle.

Hergott Shepard Residence, Beverly Hills, CA, 1999. **Michael Maltzan Architecture. Michael Maltzan. b** Levittown, Long Island, NY, 1959.

Agosta House Patkau Architects

Sited along the ridge of a meadow and surrounded by a wilderness of fir trees on three sides but open to the northwest with panoramic views of fields and distant waterways, this futuristic farmstead is a reinvention of the traditional ranch-style homes that have been associated with American identity since the 1930s. Its low-rise structure is based on a rectilinear plan and simple section with certain volumes pulled out to create programmatic exterior spaces and an enclosed forecourt, the walls and roofs sloping in response to the site's gentle slope. Galvanized-steel cladding protects the exterior from extreme weather and potential forest wildfires, while the heavy timber frame, of local Douglas fir, is left exposed within. For over twenty-five years John and Patricia Patkau have designed a diverse range of buildings across the northern states of America as well as their native Canada. They have received numerous awards, including the American Institute of Architects National Honor Award for Agosta House in 2005.

Agosta House, San Juan Island, WA, 1996–2000. Patkau Architects. Michael Cunningham. b Calgary, Alberta, Canada, 1955. John Patkau. b Winnipeg, Manitoba, Canada, 1947.   94
Patricia Patkau. b Winnipeg, Manitoba, Canada, 1950.

Tubac House Rick Joy

Clad in weathered steel, its rich ochre colour harmonizing with the desert landscape, the Tubac House is sunk into a hillside, only the tops of its two volumes visible from the road. This house is designed to appear like a natural occurrence in the landscape without compromising its function and beauty. The two main structures enclose a courtyard which, like an oasis, provides an unexpected sensory experience and the use of sliding glass panels allows outside and inside to merge. An infinity pool on the southwest side accentuates the contrast between the harsh desert and the building's clean lines and refined palette of interior materials. Windows are contained within steel boxes that are strategically placed to frame spectacular views. Joy began his practice in the early 1990s, after working for Will Bruder in New York and Rafael Moneo in Spain. His natural affinity for the desert and his vision of architecture as a refinement of nature places his work within a regional tradition and that of Native Indian vernacular building.

Tubac House, Tubac, AZ, 2000. **Rick Joy**. b Dover-Foxcroft, ME, 1958.

Lucy House Rural Studio

Rural Studio, based at Alabama's Auburn University, was founded in 1993 by Samuel Mockbee and Dennis Ruth to encourage students to consider social and environmental responsibilities as part of architectural practice. The students live within Hale County's impoverished rural communities, working on projects, from design to completion, in consultation with residents. The buildings are based on simple models typical of the Deep South — sheds, trailers and barns — and discarded or donated materials are used for construction. The walls of this family home are made from 72,000 carpet tiles; stacked to form a colourful striated structure, the tiles are held together by steel rods, which also support the deep overhanging roof. The single-storey living space leads into an idiosyncratic, prismatic tower, made from waterproofed plywood, containing the master bedroom above and a concrete family room/tornado shelter below. In 2004 Lucy House received an AIA Pioneer in Housing award.

Lucy House, Mason's Bend, AL, 2001–2. **Rural Studio**, Auburn University, founded by **Samuel Mockbee**. **b** Meridian, MS, 1945. **d** Jackson, MS, 2001.

Goodman House Preston Scott Cohen

Immediately recognizable as a traditional gable house, Goodman House is a radical reinterpretation of an American vernacular classic on a grand scale. Encased within the wooden-clad exterior is the restored timber frame of a Dutch barn built in the 1800s in the Mohawk Valley. A load-bearing steel structure, sitting between the curtain wall and the historic timber frame, allows a loose relationship between the exterior, its openings and the interior. It also allows for the partitions that usually stabilize barn structures to be removed so that the interior is open, with other living quarters housed in a two-storey side section. The 48 windows are distributed in a seemingly anarchic pattern, but offer views of surrounding mountains, and a 3 m (10 ft) wide breezeway is cut through the barn's width. Cohen extends the Modernist legacy of radical gable houses initiated by Venturi and McKim Mead & White. His trademark is the manipulation of space to resolve tensions between clients' specifications and awkward sites.

Goodman House, Pine Plains, NY, 2001–4. **Preston Scott Cohen**. b Asheville, NC, 1961.

Hill House Johnston Marklee & Associates

Perched on the edge of Santa Monica Canyon, Hill House's dramatic impact results from maximizing its volume while minimizing its footprint. Using computer software to generate the swelling and tapering volume, the architects have overcome the constraints of an awkward site and strict planning regulations for a densely populated area.

The house's modest dimensions are in keeping with the surrounding, small-scale dwellings but, like Los Angeles's Case Study Houses by Charles Eames, Pierre Koenig and Raphael Soriano, extreme invention produces dynamic form. A seamless polymer-based skin unites walls and roof, creating one complete object into which deep openings are

cut without interfering with the volumetric whole. The entrance facade, designed for privacy and to shut out traffic noise, features an upper level that cantilevers out over a recessed entrance and garage, and is in stark contrast to the expansive open interior, which opens up at the rear to frame panoramic views of the canyon.

Hill House, Pacific Palisades, CA, 2004. **Johnston Marklee & Associates**. **Sharon Johnston**. **b** Santa Monica, CA, 1965. **Mark Lee**. **b** Hong Kong, China, 1967.

Delta Shelter Olson Sundberg Kundig Allen Architects

Conceived as a weekend retreat and set on the flood plain of an alpine river valley, the design of Delta Shelter was determined by its location, extreme weather conditions, security and the client's love of outdoor activities. Clad in weathered steel, stilts lift the cabin off the flood plain. Four heavy-gauge, double-height steel shutters, which are operated using a crank wheel inside, seal off the retreat when unoccupied and during bad weather. When the panels are slid open, the cabin is transformed into a watchtower with 360-degree views. With storage and parking at ground level and two elevated storeys of living space finished with low-tech materials such as plywood, the simplicity and functionality of this compact structure is reminiscent of the pioneer's log cabin, although its form is far from traditional. Lead architect Tom Kundig's work includes residences, cultural institutions and commercial builds, and he is internationally renowned for his affinity with the landscape of the American West.

Delta Shelter, Mazama, WA, 2005. **Olson Sundberg Kundig Allen Architects**. **Jim Olson**. b WA, 1940. **Rick Sundberg**. b WA, 1942. **Tom Kundig**. b CA, 1954. **Scott Allen**. b WA, 1953.

Solar Umbrella Pugh + Scarpa Architects

Every aspect of Solar Umbrella has been devised with economy and sustainability in mind. Lawrence Scarpa and Angela Brooks created a house for their family by remodelling a run-down 1920s bungalow sited on a Venice through lot. To the rear was added a spacious living space with a cantilevered master suite upstairs. Materials are sustainable, durable, low maintenance and locally sourced: recycled steel cladding, chipboard and pulped newsprint walls, recycled plastic pellet screening and a *brise-soleil* of industrial bristles. The sheltering canopy of solar panels, its structure inspired by Paul Rudolph's iconic Umbrella House of 1953, is the key design feature and provides almost all the family's electricity as well as blocking out the sun. In addition, cross-ventilation cools the house, skylights and glass sliders make the most of natural light, and all rainwater is reused. Blurring the transition between inside and outside, Pugh + Scarpa have reinvigorated the California Modernist tradition.

Solar Umbrella, Venice, CA, 2002–5. **Pugh + Scarpa Architects**. Gwynne Pugh. **b** Cardiff, Wales, 1953. **Lawrence Scarpa**. **b** Farrockaway, NY, 1959. **Angela Brooks**. **b** New York, NY, 1959.

Loblolly House Kieran Timberlake Associates

Named after the tall pine trees that surround it, Loblolly House has been described as being at one with its environment — its very foundations are tree trunks that have been sunk into the soil. The prefabricated, wooden and aluminium structure can be dismantled as quickly as it was constructed and without leaving any physical traces.

Three forest-facing facades are clad in overlapping vertical timber strips, which are pierced with occasional slivers of glass, effectively camouflaging the house, while the fourth elevation is open to Chesapeake Bay. Established in 1984, Kieran Timberlake Associates remains at the forefront of environmentally responsible architecture, considering

sustainable design as essential rather than a preference. Using renewable and locally sourced materials, harnessing natural light and heat, and striving to minimize construction waste, they also aim to reinvent the home around contemporary needs, rather than perpetuating preconceptions inherited from vernacular traditions.

Loblolly House, Taylors Island, MD, 2006. **Kieran Timberlake Associates**. **Stephen Kieran**. b USA, 1951. **James Timberlake**. b USA, 1954.

Sagaponac House Stan Allen Architect

Part of a 34-lot residential development in the Hamptons designed by a group of architects from the 1990s onwards, which aimed to re-examine the house as a building type and adapt it to modern-day flexible living, Sagaponac House is a light and airy reinterpretation of the traditional Saltbox model. The vernacular idiom is echoed in the active roofline and use of traditional materials including lapped cedar cladding, which wraps around the roof monitors, walls and decking blurring the distinctions between house and surroundings. This dialogue is reiterated by regularly distributed large windows and skylights, and a wide opening that connects the entrance and pool terrace at ground level. The house comprises two wings joined by an enclosed first-floor bridge, with a double-height living space at the centre of the larger volume. Since establishing his practice in 1990, Allen has built a number of residences. His pared-down reinvention of a traditional house form can be compared with that of Edward Larrabee Barnes.

Sagaponac House, Southampton, Long Island, NY, 2007. **Stan Allen Architect. Stan Allen. b** CO, 1956.

Villa NM UN Studio

Villa NM nestles on a sloping plot and its twisted form in dark concrete and glass is an example of UN Studio's pioneering work in radicalizing Modernist design methods by devising new models of spatial organization. Their first residence in the United States, the house responds to the challenging site with a pragmatism characteristic of this internationally acclaimed Dutch practice. A box-like volume separates into two distinct entities: one seamlessly follows the downward slope; behind, the other rises above the ground to create a covered parking area and split-level interior. Inside, the bifurcated structure allows fluid circulation through various zones whose white sweeping walls and floors morph one into the other around a central staircase. Despite its eerie and seductive quality, the house has a sympathetic relationship with its environment, its mirror glass reflecting trees and sky. As the architect explains, 'at times the house can almost disappear into the landscape, and then re-emerge from a different viewpoint'.

Villa NM, Upstate New York, NY, 2000 – 7. **UN (United Net) Studio**. **Ben van Berkel**. b Utrecht, The Netherlands, 1957. **Caroline Bos**. b Rotterdam, The Netherlands, 1959.

Glossary

Adam Style

A **Neo-Classical** style of architecture and interior design based on the work of Robert Adam, an influential British architect known for his beautifully detailed interiors and furniture design. Adam's work dominated British taste in the late eighteenth century and was characterized by subtle detail, clarity of form and refined colour schemes. His influence spread to all corners of the globe and the style was especially popular in post-revolutionary America, where it developed into the regionalist **Federal** style.

Adobe

An ancient building material made of unburned or sun-dried mud-bricks, often mixed with straw. Adobe construction dates from the fifth millennium BC and is still used in Africa, Central Asia, Mexico and southwest America.
See pages 5, 72, 82 and 87

Antebellum

Literally meaning 'before the war', this term refers to architecture in the American South that was built before the Civil War of 1861–5 and stylistically is characterized by the grand and elaborate plantation houses of the pre-war South, many of which featured balconies, columns and pillars, covered porches and symmetrical facades.
See page 17

Architrave

A beam or lintel extending from one column to another; the architrave is also the lower division of an **entablature**, below the **frieze** at the top of a column. (See Orders)

Art Deco

A style of architecture and design fashionable in Europe and America in the 1920s and 30s, also known as **Moderne**. A reaction to the curvilinear forms of **Art Nouveau**, Art Deco favoured rectilinear shapes, particularly stepped patterns and chevrons, and used rich materials and primary colours. The style takes its name from the popular Exposition des Arts Décoratifs et Industriels Modernes in Paris in 1925.

Art Nouveau

A highly decorative form of art, architecture and design, prevalent in Europe and America at the turn of the nineteenth century, which began as a deliberate move away from the imitation of Classical forms, to embrace the new and the modern. It is characterized by flowing sinuous lines, taking inspiration from foliage, blooms, roots and stems, often in symmetrical but abstract compositions. The style included many regionally distinct manifestations: Jugendstil (Germany); Style Moderne (France); Stile Liberté (Italy); **Modernisme** (Spain); Nieuwe Kunst (The Netherlands) and Sezessionstil (Austria).

Arts and Crafts

An influential, late nineteenth-century English movement that sought to re-establish the ideals of craftsmanship which were increasingly threatened by mass-production. William Morris was the key exponent, designing hand-crafted wallpaper, stained glass, printed textiles, carpets, tapestries and furniture. The aesthetic and social philosophy of the movement were inseparable and had a profound effect on many architects. The style was taken up in The Netherlands, Germany, Belgium, Austria and the United States, where regionalist variations developed.
See pages 26, 27 and 38

Ashlar

Smooth-faced, square-edged masonry, laid in horizontal courses with vertical joints.

Atrium

An internal space rising through the full height of a building with rooms opening onto it, which developed from the Roman courtyard house. Widely used in modern architecture, it takes the form of a large, glass-covered, naturally lit space.

Balloon-frame

Timber-frame construction used in American domestic architecture, in which the vertical structural wall elements rise from the ground through to the roof, past the intermediate floors.
See pages 24 and 97

Baluster/Balustrade

A baluster is a row of vertical posts supporting a handrail. The balustrade is the entire handrail assembly, including all its constituent parts.
See page 10

Bauhaus

A German design school whose ideals and aesthetics had a profound influence on twentieth-century architecture. Founded in Weimar in 1919, the school became a focus for avant-garde and left-wing theories of architecture and design based on **Arts and Crafts** and **Deutscher Werkbund** principles of integrating art, design and architecture. The school moved to Dessau in 1926 into a new building designed by Walter Gropius. With the increasingly hostile political climate under the Nazi Party, the school closed in 1933. Many of the influential Bauhaus teachers, including Gropius, Marcel Breuer and Mies van der Rohe, emigrated to the United States, where their ideas found fertile ground in schools of architecture such as Harvard and Chicago's Illinois Institute of Technology.
See pages 43, 49 and 66

Beaux-Arts

A **Classical** style developed by the École des Beaux-Arts in Paris in the nineteenth century. Characterized by grandness and a predilection for harmonious proportioning, the style dominated fashionable taste in France and the United States in the two decades prior to World War I. The school became an internationally renowned teaching centre and trained many important architects of the time.
See pages 22, 23, 29, 30 and 40

Belvedere

A small room built on a roof or placed in a landscape specifically for the enjoyment of a view. Also called a gazebo or summerhouse.

Brownstone

Dark brown sandstone found in eastern United States. It was used extensively in the nineteenth century for the construction of New York terrace houses, called 'brownstones'.
See pages 37 and 89

Brutalism/New Brutalism (also Neo-Brutalism)

The term Brutalism was originally used to describe Le Corbusier's work in the period after 1950, where he used rough, exposed concrete finishes. In the UK, Alison and Peter Smithson — influential architects and theorists — used the term New Brutalism to describe their attitude of uncompromising rigour and intellectual clarity. By the 1960s the term was used globally to refer to any concrete building deemed to be brutal in appearance, whether or not it had any conceptual similarity with the Smithsons' theories.

Caisson

A structural element, or chamber, driven into the ground to facilitate building below water level. The term also refers to sunken ceiling panels.
See page 55

Cantilever

A horizontal element, such as a balcony, canopy or eaves, projecting from the vertical face of a building, supported only by the wall to which it is attached.
See pages 29, 38, 43, 55 and 98

Carpenter Gothic

A style of architectural detailing and picturesque wooden features incorporating **Gothic** motifs that was predominant in American domestic architecture during the nineteenth century. The **Gothic Revival** style spread across the United States in the nineteenth century, and builders and carpenters applied Gothic elements, such as pointed arches, steep gables and towers with scrolled ornament and lacy trims, to traditional, vernacular wooden structures, mainly houses and churches. Alexander Jackson Davis was a key exponent.
See pages 16 and 18

Case Study Program

A programme established in 1945 by John Entenza, editor of the US journal *Arts and Architecture*, to promote good innovative design. The Case Study experiment aimed to produce low-cost, steel-frame prototypes for houses in direct response to the post-war conditions and environment of southern California.
See pages 44, 48 and 55

Cast stone

Stone aggregate combined with cement and poured into a mould. It is often used in masonry construction in place of solid stone.

Chicago School

A group of architects working in Chicago in the late nineteenth century. They produced pioneering work with high-rise buildings using new technology and materials, such as the lift (elevator) and light-weight, steel-frame construction. A key exponent, Louis

Sullivan's Schlesinger & Mayer Department Store (1899, now Carson Pirie & Scott) embodies the school's achievements, with its skeletal structure and horizontal windows.
See page 29

Classical (also Classicism)

The term applied to architecture based on Greek and Roman antiquity. Prevalent during the Italian Renaissance, Classical theories of architecture were developed after the re-discovery of the treatises of Vitruvius (46–30 BC). In the seventeenth century, a more severe form of Classicism was evident, followed in the eighteenth century by a revival of Italian Renaissance architecture, including **Palladianism**. In the late eighteenth century, a reaction to the perceived excesses of Baroque re-established principles based on laws of nature and reason, and attention was again given to the use of archaeologically correct details. In the nineteenth century, a freer, more picturesque style emerged in Europe and the United States, which was designed for effect rather than pursuit of a rule-book perfection. By the early twentieth century, a reactionary movement once again changed the nature of Classicism and **Neo-Classicism** became the dominant style. From the mid-twentieth century, various forms of contemporary architecture based on Classical precedence represented a reaction to the dominance of **Modernism**. (See Post-Modern)
See pages 12, 15 and 69

Clinker brick

An economical and structurally efficient building brick made from the burnt and fused ash from a furnace.
See page 27

Colonial

Between 1600 and 1800 with the colonization of North America, European settlers brought a variety of building traditions from their home countries. Using local materials and techniques, the pioneering settlers adapted these, which led to the emergence of three major colonial architectural traditions: British Colonial along the northeastern coast, as exemplified by the **saltbox** houses of New England and a later generation of **Georgian Colonial** houses; **French Creole** architecture by the French colonists in the Mississippi Valley; and Spanish Colonial or **Mission Style** buildings as seen in California, Florida and the Southwest.

Composite *see* Orders

Corbel/Corbelling

A projection from the face of a wall to support a load such as an arch, beam or parapet. Corbelling is a series of continuous courses of brick or masonry, where each course **cantilevers** over the one below to form an arch, vault or dome. (See Roof)

Corinthian *see* Orders

Cornice

The cornice forms the top projecting part of an **entablature**. The term is also used to mean any projecting ornamental moulding applied to the top of a wall, column or building. (See Orders)

Corten (also Cor-Ten, Weathering Steel)

A steel alloy which does not rust. Rather, it oxidizes slowly to a dull orange-brown colour, resulting in a high-wear, protective surface.
See pages 80, 95 and 99

Craftsman

Following a nineteenth-century US tradition of bungalows (a single-storey house with an encircling porch), the Craftsman Style was developed by American architect brothers Charles and Henry Greene. The style reached its apogee in their work, which was typically of timber construction with elegant joinery and exposed beams, low-pitched **gabled** roofs and overhanging eaves, all designed and built with a concern for hand-crafted workmanship.
See page 27

Cupola

A small vaulted or domed space at the top of a larger dome, or a concave ceiling over a circular or elliptical room.

Curtain wall

Historically, the side wall of a building, spanning between the buttresses of a church, or the protective towers of a fortification. In modern architecture, a non-load bearing wall or 'skin', often of steel and glass, covering the building's structural framework.

Deconstructivism (also Deconstruction)

Beginning in the 1980s and popular in Europe and the United States, Deconstructivism was an architectural experiment based on ideas from contemporary French philosophy. While sharing stylistic similarities with Russian Constructivism, Deconstructivism was concerned with ideas such as the fragmentation and dislocation of modern cities. Buildings are characterized by complex fractured shapes, the breaking of continuity between inside and out and a general appearance of instability.
See pages 62 and 67

Deutscher Werkbund

A German organization founded in 1907 to improve the design of products through the co-operative integration of art, craft and manufacturing. The Werkbund was influential in industrial design, particularly after their Cologne exhibition in 1914 which featured buildings by Walter Gropius and Henry van de Velde. The experimental Weissenhofsiedlung housing estate in Stuttgart followed in 1927, showcasing houses by Le Corbusier and Mies van der Rohe, among others. By the 1930s their ideas were taken over by Walter Gropius who used them as the intellectual corner-stone for the **Bauhaus** School. The organization disbanded in 1934.

Domestic Revival

This nineteenth-century style saw a revival of **vernacular** English domestic architecture. Notable for its picturesque compositions, it is characterized by **mullioned** windows, timber-framing, lead-light glass, tall chimneys and **gabled**, tiled roofs.
See page 20

Doric *see* Orders

Dormer *see* Window

Elevation

An accurately scaled, two-dimensional drawing of any vertical surface of a building, internal or external. Also used to refer to the **facade** of a building. (See Plan & Section)

English Cottage Style *see* Carpenter Gothic

Entablature

The upper part of an **Order** above the column, consisting of an **architrave**, **frieze**, and **cornice**.

Facade

The exterior face or **elevation** of a building, commonly the front.

Faience

Glazed earthenware — often decorated and coloured — used for face-work, usually as large, structural blocks.

Fascia

A plain horizontal band or stripe applied to the upper part of a wall.

Federal

Coinciding with the establishment of a Federal Government in the United States in 1789, the term refers to the architecture of this time until circa 1830. Essentially **Neo-Classical**, the style drew on the work of British architect, Robert Adam, and concurrent French styles. (See Adam Style)
See pages 10, 11, 14 and 32

French Creole *see* Colonial

Frieze

The frieze is the middle division of an **entablature**, between the **architrave** and the **cornice**. It is also any strip of decoration at the top of an interior wall below the cornice. (See Orders)

Functionalism

An architectural principle adopted by various twentieth-century groups, including the **Deutscher Werkbund** and the **Bauhaus**, which insisted that the form of a building should derive directly from its function. Functionalism was first promoted by Viollet-le-Duc and Louis Sullivan in the nineteenth century. While incorporating economic, social and political concerns to reform society through architecture, extremist interpretations of Functionalism insisted that artistic expression and aesthetic pleasure were to play no part in the design of a building. Buildings were characterized by white planar compositions and the extensive use of steel and glass.
See page 29

Gable

The triangular upper part of a wall at the end of a pitched **roof**. A Dutch gable has curved or scrolled sides and a pediment at the top.

Georgian

Architecture built during the reigns of the four King Georges of England (1714–1830). The term is used to refer to stripped down, **Classical** domestic architecture characterized by plain **mullioned**, sashed windows and doorways topped with fanlights. In the United States Georgian style buildings were popular in the early colonies, where the style became known as Colonial Georgian.
See page 9

Georgian Colonial *see* Colonial

Gothic

A style of architecture also known as Pointed, that dominated European building from the twelfth to the sixteenth centuries. It is characterized by pointed arches, columns made up of clustered shafts, ribbed vaults, elaborate window tracery and most of all by an essentially vertical emphasis.

Gothic Revival

An architectural movement of the late eighteenth and nineteenth century to revive the medieval **Gothic** style. Gothic Revival buildings imitated the great cathedrals and castles of Europe and the movement had significant influence throughout the United Kingdom and the United States, as well as the rest of Europe. In the United States, wood-framed 'Gothic Revival' homes became the country's dominant style in the mid-1800s. (See Carpenter Gothic)
See pages 16 and 18

Greek Revival

A phase of **Neo-Classicism** from the mid-eighteenth century that employed archaeologically correct details from ancient Greek architecture, which only became known in the West around 1750. At first regarded as primitive, early admirers saw an unblemished purity in the straightforward simplicity of the ancient buildings. The style was widely used, particularly in the United States and Britain.
See page 15

High-Tech

An architectural approach that began in Britain in the 1970s, which emphasized the engineering aspects of contemporary building technologies. High-Tech buildings celebrate their services and structure by exposing them to view. Notable examples are the Waterloo International Terminal (1993) by Nicholas Grimshaw & Partners, and the Centre Georges Pompidou (1977) by Renzo Piano and Richard Rogers.
See page 44

Ionic *see* Orders

International Style (also International Modern)

The term International Style (synonymous in the United States with the European **Modern Movement**) was first coined by Philip Johnson in 1932 in connection with an influential exhibition at the Museum of Modern Art in New York. The exhibition featured work such as Walter Gropius's Bauhaus (1925–6), Le Corbusier's Salvation Army Hostel (1929) and Mies van der Rohe's houses at the Weissenhofsiedlung (1927). The International Style was concerned with the development of a sophisticated aesthetic, which was characterized by the elimination of all decoration, smooth white planar surfaces, large expanses of glass and flat roofs.
See pages 42, 47 and 49

Italianate (Palazzo Style)

A style of nineteenth-century architecture modelled on a type of **Classical** Italian palazzo with columns, such as the Palazzo Farnese in Rome (1517–89) by Antonio da Sangallo. The style, used extensively in Britain, Germany and the United States, was characterized by plain **facades**, **quoins**, **stucco** ornamentation and the use of heavy exterior cornicing.
See page 33

Jalousie

A type of window, or window shutter, made from angled slats of glass (or wood). The amount of air and light allowed to pass through can be controlled by opening and closing the slats.
See page 52

Loggia

A roofed arcade, gallery or colonnade, open to the air on one or more sides, serving as a protected place to sit or appreciate a view.

Mezzanine

A mid-height floor or storey inserted between two others.

Minimalism

Often confused with the 1960s art movement of the same name, architectural Minimalism is essentially an aesthetic style. Characterized by austerity, unadorned surfaces and a limited palette of materials and colours, it draws stylistically from various sources such as monastic buildings and Zen Buddhist gardens.

Mission Style *see* Colonial

Modern Movement (also Modernism)

A twentieth-century movement that disconnected itself from links to the past by suppressing all forms of ornament and historical reference, in order to establish a style appropriate to modern living. Architects relied on a scientific, rational approach, with mass-produced building components and industrial construction methods preferred over craftsmanship and artistry. The Modern Movement emerged in Europe immediately prior to World War I and culminated in the architecture of the 1920s and 30s. Walter Gropius's **Bauhaus** building (1925–6) and the **Deutscher Werkbund**'s Weissenhofsiedlung housing estate (1927) displayed the characteristic motifs of strip windows, flat **roofs**, cubic geometry

and white planar surfaces punctuated by steel and glass. (See Functionalism and International Style)
See pages 26, 36, 37, 38 and 43

Moderne

A term used in the United States in the 1930s, synonymous with **Art Deco**.

Modernisme *see* Art Nouveau

Mullion

The vertical divisions between the glass panes in a window.
See page 51

Neo-Classical (also Neo-Classicism)

An architectural movement prevalent from the eighteenth to the early twentieth centuries, that rejected the excesses of Baroque and Rococo architecture, and sought to rediscover the purity of **Classical** antiquity. An archaeologically correct application of Classicism was favoured, but there was also a preoccupation with the 'primitive' (for example, Abbé Laugier's Primitive Hut, 1753). This meshing of Classical purity and primitivism produced a style that tended towards clear uncluttered forms, pure geometry, a rational approach to design, and, in some cases, a stripping away of ornamentation altogether. Neo-Classical architecture had a tendency toward severity, starkness and intellectual seriousness. However, it also encompassed several styles (**Greek Revival**, Egyptian Revival and Empire Style), which had their own stylistic individualities but all sprang from similar architectural roots. (See Neo-Primitivism)
See pages 9, 11, 31 and 69

Neo-Primitivism

A feature of late eighteenth-century **Neo-Classicism** whereby architectural theorists, notably Abbé Laugier, argued for a strict application of the Classical **Orders**, avoiding superfluous decoration. The basis for this approach was a re-examination of the first principles of architecture, which held up the example of the Primitive Hut — a structure of four tree trunks, with sawn logs and a pitched roof — as the prototype for all architecture.

Neo-Vernacular

Architecture that draws inspiration from **vernacular** building types. A twentieth-century reaction to the pervasive canons of **Modernism**, Neo-Vernacular architecture addresses specific aspects of site and culture, such as climate, availability of building materials, *genius loci* (spirit of place) and local tradition.
See pages 77, 95, 97, 101 and 102

New Urbanism

A term coined in the 1980s and used in connection with the work of Andres Duany, Elizabeth Plater-Zyberk and Leon Krier, who promoted the idea of closely integrated urban communities with strong neighbourhood identities. The town of Seaside in Florida, United States (begun 1984), with its **Neo-Vernacular** timber buildings, human-scale streets and limited vehicle access, was a prototypical investigation into these principles.
See pages 73 and 77

New York Five

A loose association of five architects whose work was exhibited at the Museum of Modern Art in New York in 1962 and was published in the 1972 book *Five Architects*. Also referred to as the 'Whites' (due to the absence of colour in their work), Peter Eisenman, Michael Graves, Charles Gwathmey, John Hejduk and Richard Meier all presented work that displayed a formal return to the **International Style** of the 1930s.
See pages 60, 62, 63 and 71

Orders

Used in **Classical** architecture, an order is an assemblage of parts consisting principally of a column (base, shaft and capital) and an **entablature** (**architrave**, **frieze** and **cornice**), all proportioned and decorated according to one of the so-called Five Orders.
Doric: Characterized by a massive column placed on the ground without a base, terminating in a simple capital (crowning part of a column). The entablature consisted of a plain architrave and an ornamented frieze.
Ionic: The spreading scroll-shaped volute in the capital is the distinctive feature and the slender fluted shaft is used with a base. The entablature has a three-banded architrave and a frieze adorned with sculpture.
Corinthian: The most ornate of the Orders which, except for the distinctive capital decorated with acanthus leaves and volutes, is similar to the Ionic Order.
Tuscan: A simplified form of the Doric Order, the column has a simple base, and the capital and entablature above are stripped of ornament.
Composite: A variation of the Corinthian Order, the Composite Order is characterized by a capital which combines Corinthian foliage and Ionic volutes.

Organic Architecture

An elusive term that can and has been applied to widely diverse practices and forms. The early work of Frank Lloyd Wright and Alvar Aalto embodied a concept of organicism in which the parts of the building are inseparable from the whole, which in turn has an inseparable symbiotic relationship with nature. Conversely, architects in the late twentieth century have increasingly turned to scientific, mathematical and biological sources for inspiration, typically incorporating soft, flowing curvilinear shapes.
See pages 38, 57, 87 and 90

Palladianism

A **Classical** style based on the work of sixteenth-century Italian architect Andrea Palladio. Inigo Jones introduced the Palladian Style to England, but it was not until the eighteenth century that a full-scale revival of Palladianism occurred, largely due to the efforts of Lord Burlington.
See page 12

Pediment

A low-pitched gable front at the top of a Classical **Order**, often incorporating elaborate sculpture.

Perpendicular *see* Gothic

Piano nobile

The principal floor of a building, accommodating the reception, entertaining and living spaces. It is usually located above the ground floor and entered via a staircase in the entry hall. External facade treatments, such as large windows, indicate the importance given to the spaces within.

Picturesque

An eighteenth-century English concept that contrived to place buildings and landscapes in overtly painterly compositions. Picturesque compositions often incorporated real or contrived natural features, topographical decoration, pastoral scenes and real or sham ruins. (See Carpenter Gothic & Romanticism)
See page 16

Pilaster

A rectangular, non-structural projection with the appearance of a column, attached to the surface of a wall, which in **Classical** architecture conforms to one of the **Orders**.

Pilotis

A French word for columns that raise a building above the ground, creating an open space beneath. Used to great spatial and aesthetic effect by Le Corbusier and adopted by architects of the **Modern Movement** as a consistent motif.

Plan

An accurately scaled, two-dimensional drawing of a building seen from above, showing the arrangement of rooms and the thickness and composition of the walls. (See Elevation & Section)

Portico

A colonnaded roofed porch attached to the front of a building.

Post-Modern (also Post-Modernism)

A term used in the 1970s to refer to the work of architects who took a reactive stance against **Modernism** and the **Bauhaus**. Also known as POMO and P-M, Post-Modern architecture favoured a pluralist, eclectic aesthetic, often incorporating abstracted or simplistic references to **Classical** motifs, such as oversized columns, broken **pediments** and colourful mouldings.
See pages 59, 65, 67, 70 and 71

Prairie Style (also Prairie School)

A style of architecture in the Midwestern United States between circa 1900 and 1916, named after designs by Frank Lloyd Wright — such as the Robie House in Chicago (1909) — which were inspired by the simple farm buildings of the American prairies. The style was characterized by low-pitched roofs with large overhanging eaves, a strong horizontal emphasis and the dominance of the hearth as the focus of the living spaces.
See pages 27 and 38

Prefabrication (also Prefabs)

A construction system in which the components of a building are manufactured and partly assembled in a factory before being transported and erected on site.
See pages 45 and 101

Queen Anne/Queen Anne Style or Revival

English architecture built during the reign of Queen Anne (1702–14), when plainness and restraint were admired qualities. Buildings featured plain red brick, tall sash windows, canopied timber doors and flattened roofs hidden behind parapets. The Queen Anne Style emerged in the 1860s and incorporated eclectic motifs such as tall, white-painted sash windows, rubbed brick, terracotta embellishments, steeply pitched roofs, large chimneys, Dutch **gables**, **balustrades**, balconies and bay windows. The style became popular in the United States in the 1880s, superseding the French-derived Second Empire as the 'style of the moment'; unlike in England, bold colours replaced white, resulting in painted exteriors often referred to as 'painted ladies'.
See page 24

Quoin

The external corner of a building, formed by placing alternating small and large stones in a vertical stack, raised from the surface of the wall to turn the corner.

Render

A finish applied to a surface, usually a wall. Render is applied wet and can be worked to a smooth or textured finish. Typical materials are plaster, concrete, mud and pebble-dash.

Romanticism

A feature of late eighteenth- and early nineteenth-century architecture that appeared as the antithesis of rational **Classical** and **Neo-Classical** architecture. Romanticism emphasized emotion, instinct, the irrational and an interest in ruins and ghosts, over rationality and reason. Allied with **Picturesque** and **Gothic Revival**, Romanticism celebrated ivy-covered ruins, lost gardens and funerary environments, all of which was cultivated by a love of melancholy and the sublime.

Roof

The following examples represent a small number of the many types of roof.
Corbelled: Continuous layers of brick or masonry, where each course cantilevers over the one below to meet at the top, forming a rough vault or dome.
Gable or Pitched: The most common type, with sloping roof planes meeting at a top ridge and with gables at both ends.
Gambrel: In the United States, a gambrel roof is the same as a **mansard** roof. Elsewhere, it is a hipped roof with a gable end at the apex.
Hipped: A roof with sloping ends rather than flat gable ends.
Mansard: Devised by French architect François Mansard (1598–1666) and particularly associated with **Second Empire**, the mansard roof has a relatively flat top slope and a steeper lower slope on each side, allowing for a room, usually with **dormer** windows, within.

Saltbox

A timber-frame house, which takes its name from the long, sloping gable/pitched roof to its rear. Saltbox houses were popular in American colonial architecture and were two-storey at the front and single-storey to the rear. (See Colonial)
See pages 7 and 102

SCI-ARC School

The Southern California Institute of Architecture is an avant-garde school of architecture based in Los Angeles, California. Founded in 1972 by Ray Knappe, the school sought to push the boundaries of architectural study and practice with an emphasis on process — the synthesis of thinking, analysing and making — and it quickly gained an international reputation.
See page 79

Second Empire

Architecture associated with the reign of Emperor Napoleon III (1852–70) in France, but also popular in the United States. Characteristics include high **mansard roofs** with inset circular windows, **dormer** windows and ornamentation, all of which contributed to a general style of wealth and opulence.

Section

An accurately scaled, two-dimensional drawing representing a vertical slice through a building to show the arrangement of spaces, walls, windows, doors and roofs. (See Plan & Elevation)

Shingle Style

Named after its use of timber shingles, a domestic style of late nineteenth-century American architecture that developed as a nationalistic response to the celebration of the centenary of the American Revolution. Based on the traditional **Stick Style** and incorporating elements of the English **Queen Anne Style**, Shingle Style houses also employed ingenious open-plan interior arrangements that anticipated the later work of Frank Lloyd Wright and Greene & Greene.
See pages 20, 22, 66 and 70

Stick Style

An American style of domestic timber architecture that evolved partly from **balloon-frame** buildings and other **vernacular** types, such as Swiss chalets and French farm buildings. Popular in the nineteenth century, the style was characterized by timber framing and cladding, wide verandas and overhanging eaves, all giving a picturesque but angular, jagged appearance.
See page 19

Stucco

Slow-setting plaster used in Roman and Renaissance architecture to achieve a very smooth finish and three-dimensional surface decoration. It was used in early nineteenth-century English houses as an economical alternative to **ashlar** and was a popular exterior finish on Spanish or **Mission Style** homes and churches in the United States.

Taliesin

Frank Lloyd Wright began construction of a new home and studio in 1911 near Spring Green, Wisconsin, calling it Taliesin after an ancient Celtic poet. When the house burned down in 1914 and again in 1925 and 1927, Wright's commitment to the house only deepened and he continued to rebuild it. In 1932 he founded the Taliesin Fellowship, offering apprenticeships to young students to work in the Taliesin studio where they assisted with every aspect of the practice. From 1937 Wright decided to build a new home and studio in Paradise Valley, Arizona, called Taliesin West which became a permanent winter 'camp' for the Taliesin Fellowship. It was built over several years by Wright and his apprentices, and remained under construction until his death in 1959.
See pages 42, 53 and 88

Truss

A timber frame placed at intervals to form the structural component of a roof.

Tuscan *see* Orders

Vernacular

A term for traditional building forms specific to a region or country, relying on indigenous building materials and methods of construction. (See Neo-Vernacular)
See pages 4, 5, 6, 13, 72, 95 and 97

Volute

The scroll-shaped form found in the capital of the Ionic **Order**.

Weatherboard

External timber cladding made of overlapping horizontal boards.

Window

The following examples represent a small number of the many variations of window types.
Bay: A window projecting out from an external wall, forming a recess in a room.
Casement: A window where the framed glass is hung on hinges, and opens either inwards or outwards.
Dormer: A window projecting from the pitched surface of a roof, having its own roof which can be either flat or pitched.
Double-glazing: A modern window in which two planes of glass are separated by an air space for thermal or acoustic insulation.
French: A casement window carried down to the floor so as to open like doors.
Oriel: Similar to a bay window but located only on an upper floor, it can be **cantilevered** or **corbelled** out from the wall.
Sash: A double- or triple-hung window where the framed glass panes are raised and lowered vertically by cords with counter-balancing weights.

Directory

House opening times may be subject to change and access may be limited during restoration work. It is advisable to check the times and dates of opening prior to visiting or making travel arrangements. Private houses and vernacular dwellings are not listed, unless they are open to the public.

California

Eames House 1949
Chautauqua Boulevard, Pacific Palisades
This is a private residence; however, self-guided visits to the exterior & grounds are available to the general public by appointment only
www.eamesfoundation.org

Eichler Home 1950s
Various locations in San Francisco Bay area & Marin County
Tours of Eichler Homes operate annually and Eichler Homes can be purchased
www.eichlerforsale.com

Gamble House 1909
Westmoreland Place, Pasadena
Open for guided tours, Thurs to Sun, 12pm to 3pm
Closed New Year's Day, Easter Sunday, 4 July, Thanksgiving & Christmas Day
www.gamblehouse.org

Hearst Castle 1947
Hearst Castle Road, San Simeon
Open for tours daily, usually from 8.20am to 3.20pm
Closed Thanksgiving, Christmas & New Year's Day
www.hearstcastle.com

Kings Road Studios 1922
Schindler House/MAK Center for Arts & Architecture, North Kings Road, Los Angeles
Open Wed to Sun, 11am to 6pm
www.galinsky.com/buildings/schindlerstudio

Painted Ladies 1895
Steiner Street, San Francisco
Pacific Heights Walking Tours on Sundays at 12.30pm; contact the San Francisco Tourist Office

Colorado

Cliff Palace 1200s
Mesa Verde National Park, Mesa Verde
Ranger-led tours available, early Apr to early Nov. Tickets must be purchased from The Far View Visitor Center,

open daily, Apr to Oct, 8am to 5pm
www.nps.gov

Connecticut

Glass House 1949
The Glass House Visitor Center, Elm Street, New Canaan
Tours run annually from Apr to Oct,
www.philipjohnsonglasshouse.org

Mark Twain House 1874
Farmington Avenue, Hartford
Open daily, Mon to Sat, 9.30am to 5.30pm; Sun, 12pm to 5.30pm
Closed Tues from Jan to Mar, 1 Jan, Easter Sunday, 4 July, Thanksgiving & Christmas
www.marktwainhouse.org

District of Columbia

The White House 1800
Pennsylvania Avenue NW, Washington
Self-guided public tours are available, Tues to Sat, 7.30am to 12.30pm, excluding federal holidays. Requests must be submitted through a Member of Congress
Closed Sun & Mon
www.whitehouse.gov

Florida

Umbrella House 1953
Lido Shores, Sarasota
Visits by appointment; see website for details
www.umbrellahouse.com

Vizcaya 1917
Vizcaya Museum and Gardens, South Miami Avenue, Miami
Open daily, 9.30am to 4.30pm, except Christmas
Guided tours available; group tours by appointment
www.vizcayamuseum.org

Illinois

Farnsworth House 1950
River Road, Plano
Open for tours, Apr to Oct, Tues to Sun, 10am to 3pm
Closed Mon, Easter, Labor Day and 4 July
Advance reservations are required for all admissions
www.farnsworthhouse.org

Indiana

J Irwin & Xenia Miller House & Garden 1957

5th Street, Columbus
Open Apr to Sept; contact for details

Kentucky

Centre Family Dwelling House 1834
Now part of the Shaker Village at Pleasant Hill, Lexington Road, Harrodsburg
Open daily, Nov to Mar, 10am to 4.30pm; Apr to Oct, 10am to 5pm
Closed 24 & 25 Dec
www.shakervillageky.org

Louisiana

Brevard-Mmahat House 1857
First Street, Garden District, New Orleans
Walking tours of the Garden District available
www.neworleans.com

Massachusetts

Allen House 1722
Now a museum run by Historic Deerfield in Old Main Street, Deerfield
Open daily, 9.30am to 4.30pm
Closed Thanksgiving & Christmas
www.historic-deerfield.org

Harrison Gray Otis House 1808
Now Otis House Museum, Cambridge Street, Boston
Open Wed to Sun, 11am to 4.30pm
Tours on the hour and half hour
www.historicnewengland.org

Michigan

Wichita House 1946
Now located at the Henry Ford Museum & Greenfield Village, Oakwood Boulevard, Dearborn
Open daily, 9.30am to 5pm
Closed Thanksgiving & Christmas
www.hfmgv.org

Mississippi

Longwood 1861
Lower Woodville Road, Natchez
Open daily, 9am to 5pm

Montana

Tipi 1900
The Blackfoot Nation, Bear Chief's Lodge, Browning
Contact the Blackfoot Nation with all tourism enquiries
www.blackfoot.org

New Mexico

Nautilus Earthship 1996
Greater World Community, Taos
Open daily, 10am to 4pm; please call for holiday hours
The Nautilus Earthship is available for short-stay accommodation — details on application
www.earthshipbiotecture.com

Taos Pueblo Houses 1225
Taos Pueblo, World Heritage Site
Open daily, except for ceremonial occasions, 8am to 4.30pm
Closed late winter to early spring
Call in advance for details
www.taospueblo.com

New York

Boscobel 1808
Garrison, Hudson Valley
Open daily except Tues, Apr to Oct, 9.30am to 5pm; Nov to Dec, 9.30am to 4pm
Closed Jan to Mar, 18 May, Thanksgiving & Christmas
www.boscobel.org

Frick Residence 1914
Now the Frick Collection, 1 East 70th Street (between Madison and Fifth Avenues), New York
Open Tues to Sat, 10am to 6pm; Sun, 11am to 5pm
Closed Mon and national holidays
www.frick.org

Henry Delamater House 1844
Now The Beekman Arms & Delamater Inn, a hotel & conference centre, Mill Street, Rhinebeck
www.beekmandelamaterinn.com

Kykuit 1913
Pocantico Hills, Sleepy Hollow
Open for tours daily except Tues, 10 May to 2 Nov
Advance booking recommended
www.hudsonvalley.org

Springwood 1915
Home of Franklin Delano Roosevelt & Library, Albany Post Road, Hyde Park
Open for guided tours daily, 9am to 5pm
Closed Thanksgiving, Christmas & New Year's Day
www.nps.gov

North Carolina

Biltmore 1895
Asheville

Open daily, Jan to Mar, 9am to 4pm; Apr to Nov, 8.30am to 5pm; Nov to Dec, 8.30am to 8pm
Closed Thanksgiving & Christmas Day
www.biltmore.com

North Dakota

Earth Lodge 1500
Knife River Indian Villages
National Historic Site in Stanton operates tours of earth lodge sites
Open summer, 7.30am to 6pm; winter, 8am to 4.30pm
Closed Thanksgiving, Christmas & New Year's Day
www.nps.gov

Pennsylvania

Fallingwater 1939
Bear Run
Open daily except Wed, Mar to Thanksgiving weekend, 10am to 4pm; Dec weekends, Christmas week and the first two weekends in Mar, 11am to 3pm
Closed Jan & Feb
Guided tours available
www.fallingwater.org

South Carolina

William Roper House 1838
East Battery, Charleston
Guided house tours by advance appointment only
www.classicalamerican.org

Virginia

Hollin Hills 1949
Glasgow Road, Alexandria
Check website for scheduled open days
www.hollinhills.org

Monticello 1809
Virginia Piedmont, nr Charlottesville
Open daily Mar to Oct, 8am to 5pm; Nov to Feb, 9am to 4.30pm
Closed Christmas
www.monticello.org

Mount Vernon 1787
Fairfax County
Open daily including holidays and Christmas, Nov to Feb, 9am to 4pm; Apr to Aug, 8am to 5pm; Mar, Sept & Oct, 9am to 5pm
www.mountvernon.org

Index

The entries in **bold** are the architects and houses featured in this book.

Acknowledgements

Texts written by Iona Baird, Raul Barreneche, Karla Britton, Beth Dunlop, Kimberly Elman Zarecor, Martin Goalen, Ann Jarmusch, Helen Kohen, Virginia McLeod, Clare Melhuish, Jeremy Melvin, Aulani Mulford, Dung Ngo, Paul Oliver, Kester Rattenbury and Douglas Wylie.

Photographic Credits

Airstream, Inc: 41; Arch Photo Inc/ Eduard Hueber: 80; Morley Baer: 58; Karl A Backus, AIA: 86; Edward Larabee Barnes: 66; © CH Bastin & J Evrard: 5; Tim Bies/Olson Sundberg Kundig Allen Architects: 99; Tom Bonner: 76, 81; © Tom Brakefield/ Superstock: 15; Steven Brooke Studios: 73; © Richard Cheek for Hyde Park Historical Association: 32; Mark Darley: 84; © Thomas Delbeck: 72, 77, 83; Bilyana Dimitrova: 102; James Dow: 94; EHDD: 51; © Mark Fiennes: 27, 30; The Fort Abraham Lincoln Foundation, Mandan, North Dakota: 6; Dick Frank Studio: 62; Estate of Buckminister Fuller: 39; © Pedro E Guerrero: 43; Halkin Photography LLC/ www.barryhalkin.com: 101; Robert Harding Picture Library/Nigel Francis: 9; Robert Harding Picture Library/ Robert Frerck: 17; Robert Harding Picture Library/Simon Harris: 24; © Hearst Castle ®/CA State Parks: 40; Todd Hido: 91; Timothy Hursley: 18, 74, 85, 92, 96; Charles Jencks: 53; Howard Kaplan/Architectural Photography: 65; Balthazar Korab Ltd: 23, 45, 47, 54, 67, 69; The Library of Congress/Cervin Robinson [HABS RI,1-BRIST,18-3]: 22; © Lawrence A Martin/Artifice Images: 7; Norman McGrath: 70, 71; Moon Studio/Batista: 87; Michael Moran: 89; Courtesy of the Mount Vernon Ladies' Association: 8; David Muench: 4, 13; © David Muench/Corbis: 12; Dung Ngo/Anemic Design: 28; Courtesy Palm Breach Daily News: 35; Courtesy Pugh + Scarpa/Photo Marvin Rand: 100; Robert Reck: 82; RIBA Library Photographs Collection: 36, 37; Clark Richert: 61; Christian Richters: 103; © Cervin Robinson: 21, 29; Paul Rocheleau: 64; © Andy Ryan www. andyryan.com: 16, 20; Victoria Sambunaris: 97; Bill Sanders/Fort Lauderdale, Florida: 75; San Diego Historical Society: 26; Roberto Schezen/Gwathmey Siegel: 60; Shaker Village of Pleasant Hill, Harrodsburg, Kentucky: 14; J Paul Getty Trust. Used with Permission. Julius Shulman Photography Archive, Research Library at the Getty Research Institute: 42, 46, 48, 50, 55, 57; © Lee Snider/Photo Images/Corbis: 10; Courtesy of Historic New England/ Photograph by Arthur Haskell: 11; Eric Staudenmaier: 98; Ezra Stoller © Esto: 31, 52, 56, 63; Tim Street-Porter: 34, 44, 68; © Tim Street-Porter/ Beateworks/Corbis: 88; Bill Timmerman: 90, 95; The Mark Twain House & Museum, Hartford, CT/ Photography by Jeff Yardis: 19; View/ Peter Cook: 38, 49; Vizcaya Museum and Gardens: 33; Paul Warchol Photography Inc: 78; Yale Collection of Western Americana, Beinecke Rare Book and Manuscript Library/ Photograph by Walter McCintock: 25; Atelier Kim Zwarts: 79.

Jacket: Courtesy of the Mount Vernon Ladies' Association

728.0222
AMERICAN

Phaidon Press Limited
Regent's Wharf
All Saints Street
London N1 9PA

Phaidon Press Inc.
180 Varick Street
New York, NY 10014

www.phaidon.com

First published as *The House Book* 2001
This edition abridged, revised and updated 2008
© 2001, 2008 Phaidon Press Limited

ISBN 978 0 7148 4885 3

A CIP catalogue record for this book is available from the British Library.

Designed by Susanne Olsson
Printed in China